DATE			

TRUE
FANS

TRUE FANS

A Basketball Odyssey

DAN AUSTIN

THE LYONS PRESS
Guilford, Connecticut
An imprint of The Globe Pequot Press

The Lyons Press is an imprint of The Globe Pequot Press.

10 9 8 7 6 5 4 3 2 1

Printed in the United States of America

ISBN 1-59228-779-4

Library of Congress Cataloging-in-Publication Data is available on file.

For my family
and
for all the True Fans
far and wide.

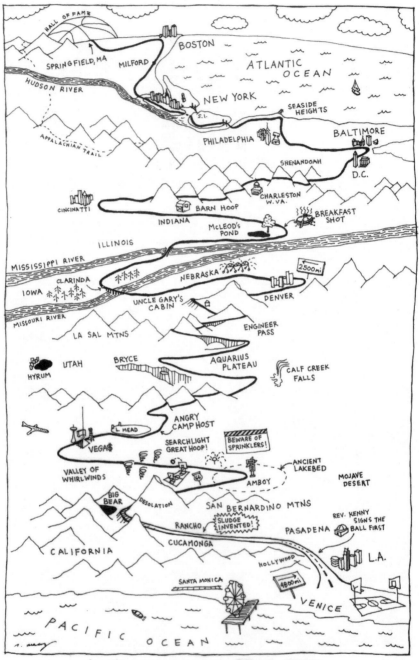

JOURNEY OF THE TRUE FANS

TRUE
FANS

1

Clint was not a pilgrim.

The only journey he was concerned about making was the fast break up and down the court. He didn't like to camp—he liked to beat his opponents to a pulp. If he couldn't get there bouncing a basketball, he didn't want to go.

That was the old Clint.

Clint and I became best friends in high school. Once upon a time basketball consumed him. It consumed him so much that it consumed me too. Clint had no desire to go anywhere. Especially by bike.

Now he bikes sixteen miles to class every morning.

Jared was not a ball player. Intellectual and clandestine, he thought Clint's time on the court was a total waste. Time better spent treating contusions or climbing mountains. He was always up for a pilgrimage, but skeptical that he'd get anything out of it.

That was the old Jared.

Jared's my younger brother by four years. Once upon a time he fled from any sort of controversy and wouldn't be caught dead on a basketball court. Now he commands a pretty mean jump shot and has even been known to skinny-dip.

The new Clint has a world map in his room with thumbtacks marking every place he's been.

The new Jared has a worn-out Spalding all-surface basketball and a wall of snapshots from around the world.

I too have a wall of snapshots and a worn-out basketball. I too am intrigued by the journey of a fast break. Just as Clint had his ball, I had my notebook and camera.

Once upon a time I believed I'd lost my one, true love.

But that was the old me.

One summer we found ourselves on our bikes in the middle of three million square miles of desert, forest, plain, mountain, river, city, prairie, and beach. Clint with his ball, Jared with his first-aid kit, me with my camera.

We flipped a coin to choose our next road. Heads. We headed east.

2

Going coast-to-coast has always held enormous romantic appeal. No matter how you do it—bike, on foot, '69 Mustang with the top down—there's something seductive about going till the land runs out. We heard legends of pilgrims on rollerblades, skateboards, pogo sticks, lawn mowers, forklifts . . . The mode of travel is as limitless as the imagination.

Think of one of the greatest pilgrimage novels of all time, *On the Road*, Jack Kerouac's tour de force. Sal Paradise and his ragtag crew live for the journey, blasting from one end of the country to the other. And when they get to the beach they spend a couple days and turn around. Why? Because there's always one more pilgrimage to make.

But what if Sal and friends had grown up in Ireland? (West coast to east coast in Ireland is about one hundred and fifty miles; coast-to-coast in North America may be four thousand.) I bet they'd work themselves into a frenzy flying from one side of the Emerald Isle to the other, and probably one day when the land quit, end up launching their stolen car into the Atlantic.

No, we are blessed with *space*.

3

The year before our trip across America, Clint, Jared, and our youngest brother Micah and I rode eight hundred miles to a bar. When you go on a pilgrimage, the shrine can be anywhere so long as it matters to you. And for us, there could be no shrine more holy than Jack and Dan's Tavern, a neighborhood watering hole owned by Jack Stockton, father of Utah Jazz star point guard, John Stockton. It sits on the corner of Hamilton and Boone in Spokane, Washington, serving up the coldest beer in town for the past forty-one years. All our lives as Utahns and Jazz fans, we'd heard stories of this True Fan Shangri-la; how locals "dance on the tables" when native son John hits a parking lot trey, how Bulls fans and other heathens are exiled from the premises at game time. It was a shrine if ever there was one. The playoffs had just begun.

The plan was to roll in during game 7, Utah versus Chicago, and watch the Jazz win the championship.

Two days into the trip, however, the Jazz were defeated by the Seattle Supersonics in the Western Conference finals. Heartbroken, but resilient, we continued on undeterred, and eight hundred miles and two weeks later arrived at the bar to a raucous, beer-crashing ovation from the jubilant pub-dwellers. To this day I wonder whether they were happy to see us or just grateful because beer was on sale all night in our honor.

Late that night Clint and I were sitting in the bar basking in the post-pilgrimage glow, chatting with folks who'd heard about the quest and had come down to see us. It had been a tremendous journey, as they always are, and we both knew right then that the next summer we would have to ride again.

Jared was in too. He was nineteen and scared to death of cities, murderers, scorpions, Winnebagos, Frosted Mini-Wheats. Jared was pre-med and had put together an enormous first-aid kit, which, ironically, he would only get a chance to use on himself.

That fall, the preparations began. Clint and I were living in a run-down apartment in Provo, Utah. I was producing and hosting a PBS television series on hiking and biking trails. I'd just graduated from film school and was starting to see our upcoming journey across America as a breakout project. Clint was in school studying to be a chaplain on a nuclear sub. "Do you have any idea what the divorce rate is for guys on a nuclear sub?" he asked me as we stood on the catwalk outside our apartment, looking across the city as the evening sun lit up Mount Timpanogos.

"Two-thirds?" I said.

"Ninety-six percent."

"Sounds like you'll have your hands full."

"I'll say." He found out a few years later that they don't even *have* chaplains on nuclear subs.

We were so poor back then that our dietary staple consisted of two loaves of homemade bread per day. I'd pop the ingredients into my breadmaker the night before and the next morning, famished, we would awake to fresh, warm bread. It was a fun ritual, but often I'd get home so wiped out from editing and shooting all day that I'd forget to put the yeast in. Clint still laments those wretched mornings, waking up and smelling fresh bread, wandering gummy-eyed out into the kitchen, and finding—instead of a plump loaf billowing over the top of the metal tin—a pitiful lump of dough in the bottom. There would be nothing to eat until that afternoon when the next batch came out.

Nothing, that is, save for some nummy Meta-Bars that made Power-Bars taste like Godiva Chocolate in comparison. The Meta-Bars were a gift from Clint's mom, who, seduced by illusions of miraculous vitality, had bought a whole crate before she realized she couldn't stomach a single bite. So she unloaded them on us. She'd also given us a few dozen cans of a horrid, no-name brand, Slim Fast sorta drink that she couldn't stomach either. Clint took out his unleavened bread frustration by winging those leaden loaves as far as he could off the third-story catwalk. One time he hit a FedEx truck. You wouldn't believe the *boom* a loaf of bread makes when it hits a FedEx truck broadside.

Those were great times. We rented a TV and watched every Jazz game. After the games we'd pull out maps and plan our route. But we didn't want to be too dialed in; a pilgrimage is spontaneity in motion. Often the greatest moments result from unexpected twists.

Initially I was thinking *big* in terms of production for this thing; I mean, *really big*. The Ark of the Covenant, our faithful bike trailer—which had lugged countless boxes of cookies, junk food, and spare tires up to Spokane—would engorge itself for this trip with 35mm film equipment, camcorders of every size, lens kits, lights, scrims . . . My budget ballooned to an inconceivable two hundred and fifty thousand dollars. The year before, the Utah Jazz organization had given us a thousand bucks for the Spokane trip. I didn't see any reason why they wouldn't pitch in a little more for this. Dave Allred, vice president of public relations for the Jazz, took one look at my budget during a meeting in February and just about fell out of his chair.

"Is this some sort of a joke?"

I didn't know what to say.

"Do you realize this is more than my entire yearly PR budget for stuff like this?"

"I didn't realize that, sir."

"Geez . . . I guess ten thousand wouldn't really help you much then, would it?"

"Not really," I said.

In the weeks that followed I began to realize that perhaps I'd made a small mistake. My budget dwindled down to a tenth of the original estimate, and just kept falling. Ten thousand dollars suddenly sounded like more than enough. It sounded like a fortune! I called up Dave, hoping the cash might still be available. Dave was cordial, wished us luck, and donated a couple of free Jazz hats to the cause.

As we neared the launch date of June first, known ever after as True Fan Day, I convinced myself that to have all our needs taken care of, to have thousands of dollars to throw around, would probably end up hurting the trip. Our goal was to see America, after all—to get to know the people and to see if they were as heroic as we'd always believed. All that other stuff would just get in the way. If you don't have to rely on the kindness of strangers, you won't. If you're cold and wet and haven't showered for a week, you'll get a hotel room. Your faith is never put to the necessary test. Looking back, the greatest asset to our trip—our only asset, in essence—was our poverty.

In the end, my film *True Fans*—the trip, the production, the editing, everything—would be made for about seven thousand dollars.

So we were going on a shoestring—maybe half a shoestring—but we were going. The question was, where? How could we possibly top Jack and Dan's?

4

For us, the Basketball Hall of Fame had always held a hallowed mystique. Located in Springfield, Massachusetts, the birthplace of the sport, it is the world's premier hoops museum, full of jerseys, championship basketballs, rare photos, and memorabilia. It is the Mount Olympus of hoops, the final resting place for the gods of the hardwood.

Without basketball, I don't know how either Clint or I would have survived high school. It was our retreat, our sacred meditation. One objective of our trip was seeking out those storied courts from coast-to-coast. Finishing at the Hall of Fame was the best way to pay homage to the sport, and make a connection between the hometown heroes we sought to meet, and the celebrated heroes of hoop, to whose shrine we biked.

Clint loved the idea, of course. Jared, however, wasn't such a die-hard fan; he wondered what was so special about a "jock shrine" anyway. I explained to him the symbolic nature of the Hall of Fame, a hall for heroes, an umbilical cord to Mount Olympus, a repository for greatness. "But yeah, you're right, it's a jock shrine."

Jared's basketball skills were lacking as well, so I advised him to begin practicing. We had to be a solid, three-man team by the time we hit the famous courts at Venice Beach, our starting point. At first he wasn't too enthused about this either. Then I warned him about "all those big, black guys down at Venice laughing at your jump shot," and Jared became incensed, practicing day and night in preparation for the trip. In our second three-on-three game at Venice before we hit the road, Jared hit the game-winning shot, earning himself the title of "game-winner" from then on out.

5

Basketball wasn't something I got into until Clint and I met in high school. But for Clint, basketball went back a lot further. "I still remember my first hoop," he told me. "I was three years old. It was a plastic, Dr. J hoop. I still remember my first dunk."

A few years after the Dr. J hoop, when Clint was eight or nine, he would play basketball for hours upon hours—as if in preparation for something. He came to the Jewish Community Center in Salt Lake City every day after school. There, he would practice free throws and crossover dribbles and three-pointers until the janitor closed the place down at ten o'clock—or a little later, since he liked Clint a lot and admired his tenacity. Then Clint would walk home, dribbling his basketball all the way, dreaming about playing in the NBA.

A lot of kids dream of playing in the NBA, but for Clint, it was different.

A couple years before, Clint's parents had divorced, and he believed, really believed as only a child can, that if he practiced hard enough and got good enough and made the NBA, his parents would be so proud they'd get back together. Basketball was his magic key. It was the way everything would be OK again. And so, he'd practice and practice, hour after hour, seven days a week. And every night, sometimes around seven, sometimes eight, his dad would slip in the back and watch him, never saying a word, just standing proudly in the shadows as his little son did the only thing he could think of to make things right.

Clint never turned around to see his dad. He knew he was there, and that was enough. It was the same concept that his on-court heroics would one day win back his family. For Clint, believing was everything.

Clint lived with his mom on the lower bench of South Salt Lake. He had a lot of friends, but when his parents divorced, he retreated, alone, into the gym and made the ball his best friend. It was on the court that he learned what it was to believe—because when he stepped onto the court, his parents were on their way to working things out, his dad was watching him proudly from the shadows, and he was NBA-bound.

Anything was possible on the sacred court.

This was the first time basketball saved him.

6

A week before the launch, everything was in place—except for a few minor details: namely, money, camera, microphone, supplies—basically everything. And to make matters worse, Clint and I were stuck in the lease at our dumpy apartment, and our landlords would not budge. This meant three months of rent, equivalent to fifteen hundred dollars—money we needed desperately to get across America. We still didn't have a camera or a microphone. The days were ticking; time was short.

Three days before we left, things started to look up. Some friends loaned us their camera. We borrowed a microphone. Two days before our departure, our landlords excused our lease. But the very day before we left, we still didn't have the binding, all-important symbol of our trip— a basketball.

But not just any basketball—an unblemished, official, NBA ball—a ball that had never been played with. We were inviting all the Heroes we met across America to sign this ball, all the True Fans, the folks who helped us out, the folks who encouraged us. One hundred days and a whole summer later, we'd present this Hero's Ball bearing the imprint of humanity to the Powers-that-Be at the Hall of Fame as a token of America, in hopes they would enshrine it.

I explained the hometown hero thing to Jared, hoping it would add meaning to the Hall of Fame, making it something more than a jock shrine. "You see, Jare, we're celebrating the common man, the unsung heroes. Their signatures will be enshrined next to the greats, in this hall of greatness!"

"It's still a jock shrine," he said. "But it is a cool idea."

Jared and I have often been at odds philosophically. While I usually defer to faith, Jared is bound to pragmatics. Jared likes proof; I like to believe. While we packed for the trip, Jared confided to Clint and me that he was starting to doubt the existence of God. The day before we left, we decided to put God to the test. We were up in Cache Valley at the time, an hour north of Salt Lake at my folks' place, making the final preps for the drive to Venice Beach, Los Angeles, the launch site.

"Jared, you know we need an NBA basketball to have people sign."

"Right."

"Well, we could buy it, but that would kill our budget. (Our budget was ten bucks a day. A new, Spalding NBA ball sets you back about a hundred bucks.)

"Right."

"When Clint and I get back from Salt Lake this afternoon, we will have a brand new NBA ball that we didn't pay for."

"How's this going to happen?"

"I don't know."

"Are you going to steal it?"

"Of course not."

"So you just expect an NBA ball to come flying out of heaven?"

"We'll see."

Clint and I took off for Salt Lake. I had an interview with a radio station that I would be corresponding with across America. I thought about asking the listeners for a ball, but chickened out.

On the way out of the studio after the interview, however, I noticed Jay Francis, vice president of marketing for the Utah Jazz, who was doing a playoff interview with a sister station and just happened to be leaving as well. I caught up to him and told him the story.

"I have a new ball in my office you can have," he said.

Jared could not entirely hide his disbelief.

"Look in the trunk, Jare, look in the trunk."

"You bought the ball, didn't you."

"I didn't buy the ball; did you buy the ball, Clint?"

"I didn't buy the ball."

We told him the story. But he just shook his head and said we got lucky.

7

While Clint was shooting his family back together, I was going on my first pilgrimages.

In the early '80s my mom and I lived in Ames, Iowa. She was getting something called a "doctorate," which to me basically meant she had to concentrate very hard on books and things, so hard that it was very easy for me to sneak up behind her and scare her to death every night before I went to bed. Back in Utah, my dad lived off the things he grew out of the garden, and sent any extra cash east. My folks were still married, but this was the arrangement they worked out so my mom could get her PhD and my dad could support the family and her education. Jared was an infant.

My mom was too busy to keep track of me, so I had free rein of the neighborhoods, even as a six-year-old. I had a blue, banana-seat bike on which I could stick myself and a few friends, and we would go everywhere. These friends of mine came from all over the world, the sons and daughters of students who'd gathered in the heartland to get an education. We'd meet up during the day and strike off on pilgrimages all over the city.

To a little kid, smallish Ames might well have been Mexico City with all its enclaves and barrios. There was a park a half block from the housing units where we lived. Here, we'd find a magic portal to another world, a tunnel underneath the train trestle. On the other side of that tunnel lay the land of "doctorates," the place my mom went during the day.

When the train whistle sounded I'd bound out the front door of our two-room apartment and tear on down to the park to watch the trains pass.

There was a tree in the courtyard in the middle of our housing project, a gigantic tree taller than anything else around. I'd climb the tree every day to watch the trains come and go and to survey my kingdom, considering new places to explore.

One day my little sister Alicia, who was living with us at the time, wanted desperately to go swimming. When a kid wants to go swimming there's just no stopping her. My mom didn't have fifty cents for the rec pool, so she walked us down to a gigantic fountain in the middle of the Iowa State campus. It seemed perfectly reasonable that fountains were built for swimming; after all, why else would they build them?

We splashed around exultantly while Mom stood guard at the fountain and smiled at everyone that passed.

"According to Vygotsky," she told me years later, "people learn about the world *through* you." Everyone who passed that day learned through my mom that kids were meant for swimming and fountains were meant for kids.

My best friend in Ames was Sherif, a kid from Cairo. Despite the fact that he took a big chunk out of my back one day with his teeth (I can't remember what brought that on), we went everywhere together.

One day Wael, Sherif's older brother who was twelve and very smart, joined the group. Wael was our enigmatic Gandalf, a wise, magical character who popped in from time to time with strange stories of exotic places and feats of magic and wonder. One time Wael had borrowed my banana-seat bike to do a bike race. He'd won the race, he said, peeling out so fast at the starting line that a cloud of smoke had gathered in the air where his tires had been. He'd won a trophy taller than he was, but it was so huge he couldn't carry it home on the bike, and had been forced to set it down. When he went back for it, it was gone. That was too bad, I thought; I would have loved to have seen that trophy.

Wael knew the neighborhoods better than anyone. Usually he would run with his older friends, shadowy faces in the twilight of childhood that kept their distance from us, as if we carried some youthful virus. But sometimes he would run with us. Today was one of those days.

"Bring your wagon," he said.

I pulled this first incarnation of the Ark of the Covenant out into the sunshine and we were off.

Now, over the course of the two years I lived in Ames, we went on many pilgrimages, and I felt I knew my kingdom pretty well. But this time, we went much, much farther than I had ever traveled before, by bike or by foot.

We journeyed past the village of aluminum-topped houses; we walked along ditches, stole through courtyards, cut across fields; followed the tracks and ambled down streets that seemed familiar but gradually became less so, until we came to a strange, broken-down part of town that none of us, save Wael, had ever visited before.

And here in a forgotten neighborhood we found a high stone wall, older than the city itself, it seemed, a wall built long ago to guard something precious. And in the middle of this wall was a gigantic, wrought-iron gate. The bars were as thick as our wrists and the lock on the gate was the size of our fists. It was such a formidable gate that it appeared nobody would ever be able to get inside to see what merited such protection. But little boys are like mice, able to squeeze through the tiniest cracks, and there was just enough room for everyone to slip through, even Wael.

I had heard the story told of Aladdin who found the Cavern of Wonders when he crept down into a cave in search of the fabled lamp. Well today, my friends and I found our own hidden and beautiful Cavern of Wonders.

The moment we slipped through the bars, we were standing in a vast fruit orchard. It was like walking through the wardrobe to Narnia. Hanging from the trees were apples and pears and peaches in abundance.

"What if somebody comes?" said Sherif.

"There's no one here," said Wael. "There never is. People have forgotten about this place."

We wandered into the orchard and were lost. Wael, as usual, had disappeared.

While my friends collected treasures from the ground, I climbed high into a tree in search of the best fruit. From my perch I surveyed the orchard and thought about Wael. He was nearly twice my age, and I saw that with age he had gained demigod abilities, but something else had begun to fade. Sometimes Wael was just as happy and carefree as we were; other times he'd sulk off and we wouldn't see him for days. He was a different person when he ran with his older friends. It seemed he joined us in an effort to decide which direction he would go.

I wondered how much longer it would be before even Wael found himself on the other side of the wall, suddenly unable to squeeze through the gate to visit the Cavern of Wonders.

We spent all afternoon in the orchard; time didn't exist for us back then. Early evening found us asleep in the shade, with golden light streaming through the trees. About this time, Wael reappeared.

"Load up the wagon," he said.

We carried armloads of fruit back through the maze, following Wael who somehow knew the way out. We filled the wagon as high as we could, then, like Aladdin filling his pockets with diamonds, filled our own with as much fruit as they'd carry.

"Follow me," said Wael.

Long shadows ran across the cracked sidewalk. The wagon made a crunching sound as it plodded along heavily behind me. The road arched up before us into the broiling underside of clouds.

We retraced our steps: through fields and neighborhoods, along ditches and tracks, across vacant lots, past the aluminum-topped villages, through the park beside the train trestle, and finally, back to my front door.

It was almost dark by the time we returned, but my mom was so absorbed in doctorate stuff she hadn't noticed.

"Look what we got, Mom!" My mom got up slowly from the card table she studied at for hours every night, rubbing her temples, and came to the door. My little gang and I stood proudly by the fruit-loaded wagon. The porch light was on; bugs zipped around, and dusk had settled. We were covered with goop, our faces sunburned, our clothes filthy.

"Where did you get all this fruit?"

"Secret," I said. Wael nodded. No one but us would know of the Cavern of Wonders.

We unloaded most of the fruit. Wael and Sherif took a bag home to their family, and the rest of my friends vanished into the early night with their pockets still bulging.

Then my mom and I sat in the little kitchen, under the dim, naked bulb, cutting the fruit into pieces and eating it. It was very quiet and peaceful, like it always is after a pilgrimage.

"I still can't believe you got all this fruit," she said. "Where did you get it from?"

"Secret," I said.

Things had gotten pretty tight for me and my mom. That same day all the food and money had run out; that afternoon, my mom had wondered what in the world we were going to eat for the next couple of days until my dad's next check came in.

But I didn't know any of that until years later.

8

With the Hero's Ball, the borrowed camera, the borrowed microphone, a microphone cable with a nasty short, and all sorts of gear, we were finally ready for the launch. We loaded everything into the back of the U-Haul and took off for Los Angeles.

In LA we picked up the last few things we'd need, like rear saddlebags, or panniers, for Clint's bike (with these yellow rain covers—"NASA-designed!" the bike shop guy said—that would cause Jared and me countless hours of frustration three thousand miles later), then we drove to the beach and unloaded everything at Venice.

Venice was a whirl of energy. The boardwalk was packed with smiling girls on rollerblades, sailing by with their hands laced behind their backs. All the shops were flung wide open, painted bright yellow and tended by sun-drenched Jamaicans, nodding behind their shades to the hushed rhythm of the ocean, or their own internal beat. Street performers swallowed glass and fire and anything else they could find. At the famous Muscle Beach, the sun massaged beads of sweat down corded arms; oblivious to the throng, and expressionless, the lifters pushed mountains of steel into the sky. At the heart of all this activity were the Venice Beach basketball courts.

Among streetball courts there are none more famous than those at Venice Beach. Spike Lee knows it: he included a beautiful shot of the Venice courts in the intro-montage for his homage to the sport, *He Got Game*. Wesley Snipes and Woody Harrelson know it too: in *White Men Can't Jump* they shoot it out at Venice throughout the film. The courts lie a sixty-second dash from the waves, and are flanked by concrete stands filled with fans, dreamers, wannabes. Courts like these sculpt champions. Locals spin tales of pro players and college standouts coming down here and not knowing what to do with the gritty, street-bred competition.

Clint asked around and had the whole pickup game system figured out in a couple minutes. "We're about five teams back," he said. "I chatted with that guy over there," Clint nodded at an old baller in a tank top with a graying goatee, sitting on the curb, tanned within an inch of his life. "He comes down here every day. He keeps things in order. Every court has somebody like him, a godfather."

Jared and I were glad he took the initiative; we were feeling a bit intimidated. "Don't worry, guys," Clint said, "it's just like anywhere else. There's a whole bunch of guys who *think* they can play, and only a few guys who can *really* play." Over on court one were a few of these guys. This was the full-court, five-on-five venue, where streamlined veterans floated up the concrete like CGI special effects.

After a thirty-minute wait, the old veteran nodded at us. "We're up, guys," said Clint.

We were joined on the court by a muscular Italian with piercing eyes, and two teenagers. Despite their too-cool-for-you air, Clint turned out to be right. The competition was more impressed by itself than anybody else was. We took the first game easily, and after a hard-fought battle and Jared's last-second heroics, took the second as well.

Now it was getting late in the afternoon. We tossed our playing ball (not to be confused with the virgin Hero's Ball) into the Ark, swung our legs over our saddles, and glanced back one last time at the ocean before the throng filled in behind us.

We rode northeast on Venice Boulevard, the ocean breeze pushing us along. We passed below the acropolis of Dodger Stadium, crossed the Los Angeles River—an acrid trickle limping down its concrete gullet to the crown of skyscrapers beyond—then wound our way through Chinatown. As the sun dipped low, we found ourselves lost in a ramble of suburbia.

And about this time, the very peak of the golden hour, a little band of kids pulled alongside us on their dirt bikes, right out of a Spielberg film.

"Where are you going?" they asked us.

"To the Basketball Hall of Fame," we said.

"Is it far?" they asked.

"On the other side of the country."

"Where New York is?"

"That's right."

They took a moment to compute this vast distance and the magnitude of the trek and then said, "We're coming with you!"

"Well, good," said Jared, "these guys are lousy company."

And for about the first half-mile they kept up. "Do you camp?" they asked us.

"We will."

"Do you eat a lot?"

"You see that trailer back there? It's full of Oreos."

"Really?"

"Hundreds of 'em."

They kept asking questions, and as we sailed along, I figured they were serious—as serious as they could be, anyway. One by one, however, the lure of barbecued chicken and homemade ice cream was just too much. They hit the edge of their kingdoms and turned around.

Maybe one day they'll go a little farther.

We wrong-turned our way to Pasadena and biked till nearly 1 A.M. before the first little miracle of the trip presented itself.

9

A few years after Iowa, when everybody was back together in the farm town of Hyrum, Utah, the family journeys began. These were the brain-children of my dad, who was the quintessential adventurer, the survivor, the ultimate Boy Scout.

At twelve years of age, he led some friends to the top of the Wasatch Mountains near Salt Lake City on a camping trip. It was mid-December. A surprise storm blew in that night, dumping several feet of snow. The authorities got word that a bunch of kids was stuck up Millcreek Canyon in the blizzard and sent a rescue team. In the middle of the night, after hours of trudging through three feet of fresh powder, the exhausted rescuers saw a light in the distance.

It was my dad and his friends. They'd heard on their transistor radio that they were "lost" and had a huge kettle of hot chocolate waiting for the "rescuers" when they arrived.

"Do you see it now? Do you see it?" He was pointing out a herd of deer, high on the hills above Blacksmith Fork Canyon, a few miles from our front door. "Just to the right of the draw." He'd guide our heads with his hand, then fit the binoculars to our eyes.

"I can't see it, Dad." We never could at first.

"You see those cliffs? Go straight down." My dad saw things with different eyes. Infinitely patient, he would help us to see, no matter how long it took.

It happened a lot. We'd be driving up the canyon in the evening, and suddenly he'd see something. We'd pull over. Leaning against the truck we'd scan the mountainside. "Oh, did you see that? That's a Lewis's Woodpecker! My goodness! I've never seen a Lewis's Woodpecker in Cache Valley before!"

My dad knew every tree, every bird, every shrub. His knowledge unlocked the world around us and enriched every journey.

Growing up, I remember countless times hearing a commotion upstairs in the early morning, and suddenly my dad would burst into my room, saying, "Get up, son, we leave for Yellowstone in ten minutes!"

Still wrapped in blankets, Alicia, Jared, Micah, Mary, and my mom and I piled into our beat-up van with the table in the back and took off. Yellowstone National Park was six hours away. We had the routine down pat: roll into Yellowstone, do a couple hikes, hit the gift shops (I was putting together a to-die-for mug collection), have dinner on the prairie or by the lake, exit via West Yellowstone, Montana at dusk, and roll back into our driveway nineteen hours later at one o'clock in the morning. These "Blitz Trips" happened all summer long. After the Yellowstone Fires of 1988, my dad, a biologist, would take us to the same "study area" each time, to see how nature was rejuvenating herself.

Crater Lake, Scotty's Castle, Devil's Tower, Mount Rainier, Glacier National Park . . . We trekked from one end of the West to the other, from Saint Louis to San Diego, from the Pony Express Trail to the Going-to-the-Sun Road. But *every* road for us went straight to the sun. We were pilgrims; we were free. The world had no hold upon us. Our old van was topping two hundred thousand miles and we never went faster than fifty-five.

And as the hours and miles passed, my brothers and sisters and I would sit in the back around the table and play a game I invented in which my siblings crafted for themselves fantastic identities with magical possessions, and I would lead them on role-playing adventures that would last for hours, days, trips, years . . . There's one story we're *still* working on. I got my inspiration, of course, from my dad, who was not only the ultimate adventurer, but the ultimate storyteller.

After rolling into camp during these family odysseys and getting snuggly in the tent, my dad would fill the blackness with stories. It was like an old magic-lantern show with characters projected in the void above us. He had an anthology of Curiosity the Bear tales, created for his children to help us fall asleep. There was *Curiosity the Bear and the Pop, Curiosity the Bear and the Popcorn, Curiosity the Bear Goes to Thunder Mountain* . . .

"Which story would you like tonight?" He'd ask us. I liked *Curiosity the Bear and the Pop* best. The thought of this bear with all the soda pop he could ever want, holed away in his secret den, was just too fantastic for me.

While backpacking through the High Uinta Mountains on our annual backpacking trip (which my dad had undertaken first alone, then with our family, every year since 1959), he'd tell us the story of Spirit Lake, his one ghost story. It scared us to death. We'd all cuddle up thinking about haunted places and ancient treks—with the enormous wilderness and its all-seeing eyes squeezing into the tent through the teeth on the zipper.

My siblings and I got so excited about these many family adventures, we'd author trip books—months in advance—discussing the wonders we were about to see. There were prologues, appendices, lists of souvenirs we hoped to find, possible routes. There's the old van, bouncing along under a gigantic sun full of smiling faces! There are the waterfalls, the mountains, the rivers, the cities!

"Where do you want to go this summer?" my dad would ask us. He'd pull out the maps and we'd peruse the vast tableau of deserts, plains, and highways.

One time we took a trip to Southern California. The first day we went to Disneyland. Disneyland was fun. The next day, we went to the ocean. Malibu Beach blew Disneyland right out of the water. None of us kids had ever seen the ocean before. I have never been happier than I was at that moment, holding my dad's hand as we stood way out in the water, bracing ourselves for the next big wave. My dad was even greater than the ocean.

And years later, when these happy days were coming to an end, one Sunday morning found my dad and me standing in the apple orchard in back of our house, an orchard he had planted twenty years before. After looking hard, he handed me the best apple on the tree, like he always did, the dew still clinging to it from the mist that had just risen.

"Live life," he told me. "Don't stay home. You can always come back—but go out and see the world first."

My dad had married young, and sometimes I'd see a bit of longing in his eyes when our journeys began. He sent Alicia off to the Peace Corps in Paraguay, Micah on a mission to Russia, my mom to Iowa, and me and Jared and our youngest sister Mary on journeys around the world. Years later, he dropped off Jared and Micah at the airport on their way to Scotland. After giving them all he could for the journey and saying good-bye at the gate, he took his favorite pen out of his chest pocket and handed it over as well. "You might need an extra pen."

My dad was the rescuer, even to the rescuers. He was always there first, with hot chocolate ready to go, always blazing the path, always preparing the way—even when the day came when he was the one who stayed behind.

And even now, with his eyes getting just a little tired from all that looking, he can still spot a deer on the mountainside ten minutes before the rest of us. He can still pick the best apple off the tree. He can still hike through meadows without a single mosquito bite, and start a fire in the middle of a rainstorm with just one match. He was our first and greatest hero; his example was the one we'd emulate on all of our journeys for years to come.

10

We were awakened our first morning by a friendly face peering over the garden wall. It was an older, Jamaican fellow who, judging by the overalls and the jangle of keys, was the church's custodian.

"Morning," he said.

"Morning," we said.

"Homeless bother you none?"

"Nobody bothered us."

The man nodded and walked off. Clint and Jared and I wiped the sleep from our eyes and got our first, daytime look at our surroundings.

Last night, at the very height of our fatigue, we'd stumbled upon this little garden tucked away behind the Christian Science Church in Pasadena. We'd pulled aside the iron gate—much smaller than the gate to the Cavern of Wonders—let ourselves in, and thrown out the bags.

The Jamaican fellow ambled back. "So nobody bother you none," he said.

"Not a soul," we said.

He nodded in satisfaction, as if he had something to do with whether we'd been bothered or not. "I'm Kenny Shaw, the caretaker of the church," he said. "When you're ready, you come in and get washed up. I'll open the bathrooms for you."

As it turned out, Kenny had already been poking around the church for a couple hours before we'd awakened. It was his job to kick us out, but he'd let us sleep in. I suppose he felt for us; he'd pilgrimaged to Pasadena from Jamaica with his family thirty years before.

I looked up and noticed that the windows to the reading room stared right down onto the garden. There were a few folks gawking at us, surprised, no doubt, to look out and see, instead of a peaceful garden with birds and rabbits, three scraggly guys crashed out around the birdfeeder.

As Kenny walked back he seemed to notice it too. "Why don't you come inside and meet your hosts," he said.

While Clint and Jared broke camp, the caretaker led me down a cobblestone path to a doorway; we entered the halls of the church and walked into a nearby office. "He just wanted to thank you for allowing him and his friends to sleep in the garden last night," said Kenny to a woman sitting behind a desk.

"You're very welcome," she said.

Off to my left through the massive windows I watched Jared and Clint roll up the sleeping bags.

"There now," said Kenny, as we walked back down the hallway. "You have friends here. If you ever come back to this place, you have friends." Perhaps this is why he let us sleep in, because whether we were friends before or later, we were friends now, and that's all that mattered.

"So, where are you biking to?"

"We're heading across America."

"Across the whole country . . ." Kenny's eyes got distant for a moment, as if he were seeing all the places we'd visit in a sudden flash. "Well, then, there's something I want you to remember on your journey," he said as we stepped outside. And he stopped me here on the cobblestone path and looked me square in the face. "Always remember, *Seek a friend, before you need a friend.*" He said the words carefully, enunciating every syllable, as if we would live or die by these words. His accent was still heavy, and I had to listen closely to understand. "Always remember this: *Seek a friend, before you need a friend.*"

Back in the garden I helped Jared and Clint load up the bikes. Then the caretaker ushered us inside the chapel to wash up and listen to the organ in the great hall. "They used to film movies in here," he whispered. "Then things got a little rough one time and that was it."

It was getting warm and we were anxious to move. Kenny stood at the chapel doors to bid us farewell, but we asked him for one last favor first. From deep within the Ark of the Covenant I found a canvas bag, carefully guarded from the sun, rain, and elements, with drawstrings pulled tight around the top. Loosening the strings, I withdrew our pristine, unblemished, never-played-with NBA basketball, the Hero's Ball that Jay Francis had given us at the eleventh hour in Salt Lake.

"We're riding our bikes across America to the Basketball Hall of Fame," I said. "We want to see if our country and our people are as good as we've always believed them to be. We're carrying this basketball with us, and we're inviting all the heroes, the True Fans we meet, to sign this ball. When we get to the Hall of Fame, ninety-nine days from right now, we'll present this ball to the Powers-that-Be, in hopes they'll enshrine it. We'd like you to be the first one to sign it."

Kenny Shaw didn't quite know what to say. I suppose it's not every day three wayward pilgrims appear on your church lawn on a quixotic journey to a far-off shrine and ask you to sign a basketball bearing the imprint of humanity.

"It would be my pleasure," he said at last. I handed him the Ball; Jared produced a black Sharpie. "It would be my pleasure," he said again, as he signed his name on the virgin leather.

When he handed back the Ball I looked at his signature. It read: *Rev. K. Shaw.*

"What does the 'R-e-v' mean?" I asked.

"The 'R-e-v,'" said the caretaker slowly, "means 'Reverend.'"

"You're a reverend?" I asked.

And the reverend said, "Yes, I am."

And this is the moment we will all remember. For in that moment, the caretaker disappeared and the reverend took his place. It was an astounding transformation, as if we'd blinked in unison and a new person had appeared. It was more than his shoulders squaring, his back straightening, more than his eyes filling with a new and even deeper caring for us, more than an electric vitality enveloping his whole body—like the billions of cells had just started humming—no, it was more: there was a radiant light suddenly surrounding him. Whether it came from heaven above, or from his heart within, we couldn't tell.

"So, God bless you all and a safe journey," said the reverend, now with perfect clarity and perfect ease. "God be with you all." He shook our hands; then the doors to the chapel opened magically behind him, and he disappeared inside.

11

Clint and I met in high school. Somehow we'd both found our way to a sheltered valley in rural, northern Utah. He was living with his dad and stepmom in the tiny hamlet of Mendon. We were freshmen, and he was the biggest jerk I'd ever met. I didn't know about all those years of practice yet, but I could see the results. Clint was a tenacious competitor and the starting point guard on our no-holds-barred freshman basketball team that everybody was talking about. "When these guys get to be seniors, the state title is theirs," prophesied fans and opponents alike.

Clint and I first hit it off during an overnight hike to the top of the razor-finned Wellsville Mountains. Friendship often begins with a pilgrimage. We sat around the campfire (me, Clint, and our buddy Brandt), high above the glittering valley, and Clint went off about some girl he'd met in our freshman German class. I'd have to get used to his ramblings; I'd be hearing about Lisa Benson for the next ten years. She was quite a coquette, it seemed, and no amount of basketball wizardry could win over her heart. Ahh, but Clint was persistent, and vowed that very night on the mountain that he would marry her one day.

Clint introduced me to the peace of the basketball court, and I introduced him to the hell of filmmaking.

Every week or two we'd run out into the desert or way up into the mountains and shoot movies. Usually they had something to do with wizards and medieval road trips. There was a lot of blood, a lot of running around in gorilla suits, a lot of falling off waterfalls. We had a motto back then: *Anything for a scene.* Clint adopted the motto as a personal mantra and acquiesced to whatever bizarre and painful scenarios I had cooked up. Like one time on the salt flats . . .

It's 90 degrees and I've got Clint crammed into a gorilla suit (he was playing a mountain troll, but it was the best I could do). He's lying face-down on the flats, motionless, as he has just been killed by Altov of Valtaria, a warrior on a pilgrimage. I'm trying to do a long pan, but I can't get the shot right so I'm doing it again and again. Around take fifteen, the heat gets so bad Clint passes out. Around take forty-five he wakes back up, completely drenched with sweat, his cheek floating in a puddle of drool in the bottom of the mask.

And I didn't even end up using the shot.

A few months later I had him submerged underwater for forty seconds at a time while this same Altov (played by Brandt) dragged his way to shore after falling off a waterfall. The water was frigid snowmelt, and Clint (playing the part of a changeling assassin this time) wore a skimpy tunic. After a dozen takes, he leapt out of the water, threw down his prop bow and arrow, and, shivering uncontrollably, proclaimed that I could find another assassin—and best friend.

Luckily, I used that shot.

Clint would take out his frustrations on me on the basketball court. We'd play for hours, games to one hundred points, five hundred points. We'd go and go. When we skipped our junior prom, we played basketball all night long. And every time we played it was the same ritual— once you step over those white lines onto the sacred court, the whole world is forgotten, the slate's clean, there's nothing to worry about—just sinking your next shot.

It was during those long, wonderful battles stretching through the seasons, years, nights, and days that Clint first told me about his childhood—

about the magic court where anything was possible. In his heart, even all these years later, he still clung to the belief that by making the NBA, he could make everything all right.

Coach Nielson, however, had other plans.

Every fall Clint and I made the annual pilgrimage to "the wall" to check the list of guys who'd made the team. We were juniors and, just as a formality—not because it would give us any new information—we ran down to check.

Clint's name was not on the list.

He stared at it for several minutes, disbelieving. He read it forward and backward. Taking the point guard position was a short, rich kid Clint could beat in his dreams. It stunk of politics. Nielson's excuse was "numbers."

Two years after Clint was cut, the Mountain Crest freshman team that could not be beat came a three-pointer away from taking the state title. If Clint had been playing, he might have made the shot that didn't go in—Lord knows he'd practiced it enough times. I guess he was just saving it up for a later day . . .

Despite the fact that the NBA (let alone varsity ball) was no longer an option, basketball had not lost its magic effect on Clint. In fact, I think a sense of relief came over him, realizing at last that the burden of making everything all right again was no longer on his shoulders. All he had to do now was make everything right for *himself.*

This was the second time basketball saved him.

12

With the reverend's prophetic blessing upon us, we struck off through Rancho Cucamonga, and then climbed above the heat of San Bernardino to the valley of Big Bear Lake. At seven thousand feet, Big Bear offered a cool retreat from the congested inferno below. We rolled in at dusk. On the hillsides above us, the cozy glow of cabins peeked through a veil of pines. Mist crept over the tops of the hills and settled on the water. Waves lapped at the banks where canoes slept. As we rolled down the quiet lane, we saw the distant lanterns of Main Street welcoming us to town. Game 2 of the finals was on, and somebody had mentioned a sports bar, Chad's, where we could watch.

We locked our bikes up outside. There wasn't a soul about. Inside, a few locals had gathered. The game was on and we kicked back to rest our legs from the ascent. But the Jazz lost, and Clint nearly got into a brawl with a couple of drunken Chicago Bulls fans. "They don't even care," he said. "If they're True Fans of the Bulls, that's one thing. But they're just bandwagon fans." In the True Fan lexicon, there is nothing more abhorrent than a bandwagon fan.

■ ■ ■

We rode around the south side of Big Bear in the starry darkness and camped at the Sorreno campground. The combination of our late arrival, our first tough climb of the trip, a Jazz loss, and the cool morning seduced us to sleep in. When we finally got up, everybody was in a hurry to move, especially Jared, who was always flustered about mileage and making sure we got to wherever we were supposed to go—wherever that was.

But we had to eat first. Peanut butter and jelly sandwiches had powered us all the way up the mountain, and we were out of fixin's, so Clint biked to the store and bought a huge, two-pound jar of jelly that fell out of a hole in the grocery bag ten feet from the picnic table and shattered. Clint stared at the jelly. Jared stared at Clint. The get-going frenzy ground to a halt.

"Guys," I said in the sobering moments that followed, "we've got all summer to get to the Hall of Fame."

Clint looked up from the mess. You'd think his favorite dog had just died. Jared was computing how much this loss was going to affect our daily budget. "All summer, guys. We don't have to be anywhere; we don't have to do anything. We can sleep in till two in the afternoon if we want. We can ride all night long. This is our trip."

It really was the jelly that broke the camel's back. We weren't used to abandoning ourselves to the road yet, and found it too easy to superimpose the habits of civilization on our trek.

"You know what I want to do," said Clint a while later, after we'd cleaned up the jelly and settled down. "I want to teach a kid to roll a basketball up his arm. Sometime before the end of this trip, that's what I'm going to do." Sitting at the picnic table reading *The Grapes of Wrath*, Jared toasted his declaration with his fourth cup of hot chocolate.

True to our decree, we didn't break camp until early afternoon. Then we headed west into the barren, Baldwin Lake half of the Valley. Unlike Big Bear, Baldwin Lake is just a scaly lakebed where a lonely whirlwind whipped around like a kid on a dirt bike. It seemed to be the only sign of life—which was too bad, because there was an obscure dirt road we had to find that would shoot us off through the desert to Pioneer Town beyond. If we didn't find this road, we'd either get lost in the wilderness or have to double back through San Bernardino.

Kelly and Rita Dills found us scrutinizing the map a few minutes later. They were tying up their horses after a ride and walked over to see if they could help.

"Oh, that road," Rita smiled. "You'll never find it."

"People get lost out there all the time," said Kelly. "It's a good thing we ran into you."

"Can you tell us how to find it?"

"We can tell you, but you'll still get lost," said Kelly.

They led us down a sandy track that was barely more than a footpath through the scrub oak. The sand was hot, red, and deep—the wheels on the Ark were getting buried. A couple times I had to stop and Clint and I would lift the Ark across an especially deep stretch. The Dills turned onto a hidden spur where we crossed the Pacific Crest Trail, and a couple miles later we ended up at a junction with a primitive dirt road.

"This is where we leave you," they said. "There's a nice campsite a few miles farther. Just go until you get to a marked forest service road, hang a right, and push your bikes up into the hills. There's water, shade; it's beautiful."

Kelly and Rita signed the Ball.

The San Bernardino Wilderness opened around us. The road was etched into the mountainside above a clear, desolate vista. We imagined the first Spanish explorers here in the 1700s, awed by the grandeur, and, I would imagine, intimidated by the harsh emptiness.

We rode down through a cathedral of Joshua trees, took the recommended spur, pushed our bikes for a mile on a chewed-up track, and high on a hillside in the evening dim, found the Round Valley Campsite. It was indeed a slice of Eden in the desert. There was a spring, a grove of trees, and a spectacular view over the valley.

Late that night we watched thunderstorms scour the expanse, lightning in their hands. Sometimes when we talk about the trip, Jared says that this is the place he'd like to return to the most, just sitting on that gentle rise watching the storms sweep across the waste like an army of fire ants.

13

It had taken some gentle arm-twisting to convince Clint to join Brandt and me on that first mountain climb back in high school. Clint had never gone on pilgrimages before and didn't want to start. As my budding best friend, however, he didn't really have a choice. A month after the hike, I planned our first, bike-bound odyssey. There could be only one destination: Uncle Gary's.

The consummate bachelor, Uncle Gary decried marriage, commitment, responsibility—he traveled the world, quit jobs when he felt like it, watched HBO all night long, spoke four languages, and had dealings with extraterrestrials; he was the embodiment of the teenage quest for independence. He was also the guy who drove us all over the place when I was making movies before I had a driver's license. He played all the villains and was killed twenty or thirty times. "I actually got to sort of like the taste of fake blood oozing out of my mouth," he told me.

To convince Clint to give the pilgrimage a try, I brought him with us on a few Yellowstone Blitz Trips, inundated him with maps and drawings and stuff-lists (not unlike those early books about our family journeys), and spun tales of how our adventuresome derring-do would be received by girls back home, namely Lisa. I think this last one put Clint over the top.

And so, our first journey together was a day trip to Uncle Gary's place in Ogden, Utah. We felt like world-conquerors, biking an inconceivable seventy-six miles, and celebrated with gallons of Coke, Uncle Gary's trademark steaks, movies all night long, and, of course, more basketball.

The following summer we embarked on a two-day odyssey, once again to Uncle Gary's. The old hermit now lived in Idaho Falls. We strapped Twizzlers to our handlebars, outran vicious hounds, and hitchhiked the last thirty miles when Clint's bike broke down. We had a glorious time, and the next thing you know we're best friends—inseparable—dreaming out the rest of our lives. I was going to film school; Clint was joining the Navy. It was the summer of 1992.

14

A lot of cross-country pilgrims visit a place called Amboy, a tiny desert town that sits right along Route 66. Decades ago Route 66 was called "the Mother Road," carrying thousands of hopeful pilgrims from the devastation of the dustbowl to the promise of California. Now, it carries mainly nostalgic history buffs who marvel at the forsaken remnants of its former glory—remnants like Amboy.

Amboy's the only place for about a hundred miles in any direction to get gas, POWERade, or a Premium Creamie. Sometimes the store at Roy's Café shuts down in the middle of the day for no reason. I suppose when it's that hot you might as well. Most trains don't stop in Amboy—they'd rather not—but those that do bring thousands of gallons of coveted water. There's no water in Amboy; locals have to pay for every imported drop. And everybody will tell you so if you ask for a drink.

"That's hot desert," said Peter, an Aussie I met in Chad's at Big Bear during halftime of the Jazz game. "And the people down there . . . be careful. You wouldn't believe the things that happen at night." Peter had come to California a couple decades earlier for the waves and girls, got old, tired, and bored, and moved to the mountains. That's his story.

Inbreeding and chemical testing are rampant around Amboy; UFOs are a nightly ritual—like a drive-in movie. Harrison Ford once landed his plane there; he was immediately mobbed by the town's thirteen residents and forced to take innumerable photos before they'd give him the bathroom key.

"Don't go to Amboy," said Brandon, late one night on top of the Sheep's Hole Summit, a thirty-mile, downhill glide from the cursed village below. Brandon and his buddy Jason had stopped to see if Clint, comatose on the side of the road after the long ascent, was dead, passed out, murdered, or asleep.

"I can't believe you guys would stop in the middle of the night in this desolate country full of murderers and inbred crazies," marveled Jared.

"That's the chance we take," they said. They were military paramedics with two weeks' leave from blistering 29 Palms. Jason was getting married in three days in Oklahoma, and Brandon was along for the ride.

"We were just passing by and we thought we saw blood on his face," said Jason.

Not blood—just chocolate from the melted Hershey's jumbo bar Clint had been gnawing on all the way up to the summit. Clint stared at Jason in his drunken-with-heat trance and smeared chocolate across his face with a greasy forearm. "Did I get it?"

It was a long summit. Desert summits don't surrender without a fight. The road doesn't ascend at much of an angle, which means you have to pedal uphill for a long, long time. What's more, the air is so clear that distances get distorted. We'd figure a mile when in fact we had ten. At night, we just had no clue. It was like we'd been reincarnated in one of those hellish, mythological torments, bound to struggle up the mountain for the rest of eternity with nothing to abate our hunger but a Hershey's jumbo bar, which just incensed our thirst.

The only indication of how far we had to go was the occasional car. Only a handful passed us all night long, but we'd watch each one desperately, keeping our eyes on those taillights, hoping to see them blink out over the top, telling us the summit was near.

"It's never going to end, is it?" said Clint, an hour from the top.

"No, Clint, actually it's not," said Jared.

Clint gnawed away on the Hershey's bar. "You know that's just going to make you thirsty."

"I know that."

He took another bite. We could hear his gums smack, they were so sticky from the dry air.

"Here comes another car." The car blasted by. We watched it until the taillights faded. "We're not even close," said Clint.

In fact, the only indication we had when we *did* finally make it was that suddenly we weren't rolling backwards anymore. "Well, Clint, you were wrong, it did end," Jared said.

Clint offered a couple Hail Marys and collapsed on the side of road. Ten minutes later Jason and Brandon's Jeep flew by.

"We were thinking of riding down into Amboy tonight and finding a patch of grass," I said.

"Ain't no grass in Amboy," said Brandon in his gravelly drawl. "I'd recommend you curl up next to a tumbleweed right here."

"The closer you get to Amboy," said Jason, "the worse it gets."

"What do you mean?"

"Well, one night I was pulling through town and I saw a cross burning in a field."

"No kidding."

"Another time, I was driving through and a guy tailed me doing ninety all the way to the interstate. Never got farther away than twenty feet off my rear—that's fifty miles."

"A couple years ago there was a murder in the big crater you'll pass on your way to town."

"And Charles Manson got his start in Amboy, so they say."

Usually you could count on Jared getting the creeps, but this time it was all three of us.

"Hey, you guys want some Fig Newtons or something? We got an extra box in the Jeep."

■　　■　　■

We set up the tent a ways off the road, amid a field of sand and scorpions. Clint slept with his U-lock, "Just in case some of those Amboyites come for us . . ."

The next morning the sun peeked over the horizon and turned the tent into a kiln. When the sun's up in the desert, you're up; it's the harshest drill sergeant around.

We packed up and pulled our bikes onto the road.

On the other side of the Sheep's Hole Summit the desert plunged before us into a panorama of unequaled desolation. Distant mountains stood like shards of broken glass cemented into the plain. The sky was bleached out, cloudless and enormous.

We sailed off the summit into a vast valley, an ancient lakebed that looked as big as Lake Michigan from our high vantage point. Along the shore massive curls of sand and dirt looked like petrified scoops of Rocky Road ice cream, monuments of a salt company's efforts down here. Off to our left rose the murdering crater Jason had told us about.

A few miles farther we rolled into Amboy, population thirteen. The town is little more than a couple of decrepit trailer houses, a post office, a deserted school, a forlorn schoolyard with abandoned swings, a boarded-up church, and, emblem of Route 66 golden days, Roy's Café.

We'd heard Roy's had air conditioning, and the temperature was already pushing one hundred and five, so we rolled up, walked in, and sat down at a table.

Despite the oddness of Amboy, I just didn't think it could be as bad as everybody said. Cross burnings? Murderers? UFOs? A little sad man came and took our order. He had the emptiest eyes I'd ever seen. A few Route 66 tourists popped in and out. We ordered shakes and burgers and supplemented the meal with more peanut butter sandwiches. The little sad man brought us our food and recounted the glory of Roy's Café.

"Anthony Hopkins was in here a few weeks ago," he said. He opened a magazine to a black-and-white photograph. "He was sitting at that table right behind you guys." Then he pointed out his own picture with Harrison Ford hanging on the wall. "Just flew his airplane in one day. He said, 'I want to visit my friends in Amboy . . .'"

"You mind if I get a couple shots?"

He shrugged.

"Have you always lived here?" asked Clint.

"Used to live in San Bernardino."

"Why did you come to Amboy?"

"I hate people," he said, walking away.

We cleaned up our shakes and I went to get that shot of Harrison Ford. While I did, the sad man approached me and told me to turn off my camera.

"Is there a problem here?" I asked. The cook looked on from the kitchen. Seemed they'd had a little chat.

"If you want to shoot anything in Amboy you've got to call this number." He handed me the card of a location management firm in New York.

"I thought you said I could shoot a few things."

"That's the number; if you don't call it first and buy a license, we'll sue you."

"Look, I'm not Anthony Hopkins—"

"You know what," said the sad man suddenly, "I think it's time for you to go. You and your friends have been here long enough."

"It's one hundred and five degrees outside—"

"Somebody else needs to use this table." He slapped down the bill. "Leave."

"Starting to sound like Jason and Brandon were onto something," said Clint as we packed up our stuff and walked outside.

It was like stepping into a furnace. There was a table with a few chairs in the shade near the gas pumps, and we sat down.

Fifteen minutes later, the little sad man came out of the building, told us to stand up, and tossed the table and chairs into a storage shed. "I told you to leave."

"It's too hot to ride."

There was a sliver of shade next to the post office—the only other shade in town. "We'll just go sit over at the post office until it cools off."

"I own the post office," he said. "I own the café, I own the hotel . . . I own this *town*."

"You don't own the post office!" erupted Clint with a surge of patriotism that a month later would nearly get him killed. But looking across the street, no flag flew from the empty pole.

The little sad man walked back inside to close up. A fat guy in a Hawaii flower shirt was pumping the last gas of the afternoon. "Guys, don't argue with him; just thank him for the water and leave. This is his territory now." It sounded like he knew something we didn't. But still, it was too hot to ride. We'd be out of water within a few miles.

We languished all afternoon in the pitiful shade by the post office as the little sad man stared us down from across the street. An hour later a car rolled up, 5-0 engine grumbling. A couple guys hopped out and met the sad man out front. They chatted for a while, glancing over at us. Then they got back into the car and drove away.

In the meantime, I went inside to chat with the post office clerk. "Oh, Amboy's the best! I moved away for fifteen years and knew I had to come back. This is the *only* place I want to raise my children. Kids need space, you know? Space."

I asked her about the UFOs.

"Not that kind of space."

I asked her about Charles Manson, murderers, burning crosses. She seemed put out that I would believe such nonsense.

"Never seen a burning cross," she said. "Never heard a thing about Charles Manson. That murder in the crater? Well, the woman went in on a hot day without water. She got heat stroke. And nobody around here has the time or energy to go chasing people across the desert." She laughed sternly, tiring of my questions.

"What about the new owners of the café across the street?" I asked.

"Oh, they seem like the nicest guys on earth."

■   ■   ■

We spent the afternoon waiting for a reprieve. Clint worked on his two-handed chest pass, bouncing the basketball against the side of the post office. Jared attempted some afternoon Sludge. In the evening, massive thunderclouds boiled up in the west and finally cooled things off.

"Let's ride."

The sun cast our shadows straight and long in front of us. We went blazing out of town like three Old West heroes. And the little sad man walked into the middle of the road, watching us until we disappeared.

15

That night it was so clear the stars looked like pieces of tinsel floating down after a football game, and so impossibly quiet we could hear the trains creeping across the desert from fifty miles away. I never dreamed during my Iowa days that those same trains rushing through the corn-fields would find themselves in a place like this, but their distant moans were strangely comforting nonetheless.

"Another scoop, Dan?"

"Why are we whispering?"

"I don't know."

Maybe we felt like they could hear us. We'd only ridden thirty-five miles out of Amboy. After dark we'd pulled way off the side of the road, made camp amid the glittering, busted beer bottle waste, and hid all our bike reflectors under T-shirts to keep from being detected.

About a half hour after we stopped, a big 5-0 engine came trawling by, doing about forty, which is about fifty miles per hour slower than everything else goes out here. We froze, waiting for the swath of head-lights to pass.

"They're looking for us," whispered Clint. The rumbling faded and we returned to our dinner.

Jared was scraping the bottom of the pot with his metal spoon a while later when headlights appeared in the distance. We threw a T-shirt over the pot and laid back on the tarp. The same car that had passed us a half hour before came growling back from the opposite direction. It was doing closer to thirty now. The edge of the headlights tickled the edge of our camp. We didn't move until the rumbling had faded completely back into the night.

16

The World Tree rises from heaven to earth. Its roots are sunk deep in the ground; its trunk rises through our perception, its branches mingle with clouds and lose themselves in the land of giants. Tree of Life, Tree of Knowledge, Tree of Wisdom—every religion, people, and culture has a different name for it. Odin hung from it; Buddha fasted in its shade. Its crown has no end in height; its roots, no end in depth.

"I've seen it, Dan," Clint told me once, a long time ago. "It's sunset and the hoop is all silhouetted, and there's two guys, just like us, shooting around. I think it might be down by the ocean, but I'm not sure. That's the hoop I want to find."

Somewhere, the World Tree rises from earth to heaven. Nearby, the Perfect Hoop awaits the seeker. Perhaps the backboard was made from a limb of the tree; probably so. It is the shrine where fathers watch their sons, where families stay together—the archetypal hoop where miracles rain down from heaven like parking lot treys.

Clint shows me a clipping he's been carefully preserving, like an image of the Virgin Mary. He cut this one and only shot of the Perfect Hoop out of a magazine years ago and has religiously carted it around with him ever since.

"The light, you see the light? It's golden, you know, that's why I think it's down by the ocean. And I think that's a seagull in the background there."

The clipping is so bleached by time most of its color is gone. But I agree with Clint—the light is golden. And it might be a seagull.

Of course he brought the picture with him on this trip, of all trips; he keeps it carefully stored between four hundred massive pages of *The Basketball Encyclopedia*, which, mercifully, I am not carrying in the Ark. The *Encyclopedia* and a library of Steinbeck, Hemingway, and Twain crowd all the space in one of Clint's panniers.

There would be many times during the course of the trip when, after rolling into camp, Clint would take out the clipping and proclaim that perhaps tomorrow we would find the Perfect Hoop. In retrospect, I think we found it again and again.

The fountain of youth, the World Tree, the Perfect Hoop—the pilgrim searches for the wormhole to transcendence.

But in order to search, one must survive. Early in every journey, the pilgrim develops a sustaining dish. It is magical fare that happens like a revelation, a freak act of serendipity. It must be easy to make and big on carbs. It is the go-to dish, the superstar—the dish to put on the stove when the trip's on the line.

"*True Fan Sludge*," Jared has since repeated to rapt audiences on countless occasions, "is made from pasta and soup packets and prepared by boiling off the water until a casseroley, sludgy mass remains."

Prophet-like, Jared called down the sustaining mysteries of heaven on a church lawn in Rancho Cucamonga our second day out. *Soup packets are cheap and give it taste. Boil off the water and retain nutrients. Casserole needs no expensive Paul Newman sauce . . .*

From that day forth, we'd eat True Fan Sludge every night. And if there were leftovers: *True Fan Sludge Cake* in the morning! While sleeping, the uneaten Sludge congeals, forming a solid mass in the bottom of the pot. We'd cut it into chunks, dunk it in ketchup, and voila!

All day long it was peanut butter sandwiches—the Ark becoming a repository of plastic knives, bread loaves speckled with mold, limitless jars of peanut butter—and every night we'd huddle around the Coleman stove, like our ancient, pilgrim forebears around Pleistocene campfires, and watch in wonder as the vat of Sludge bubbled and hissed.

In years to come the Sludge variations exploded. Divine inspiration led to the development of *True Fan Scottish Sludge*, *True Fan Shakespearean Sludge*, *True Fan Yellowstone Sludge* (the alchemy of Kraft instant cheese packets serendipitously providing its golden, Yellowstone hue), *True Fan Ranch Sludge*, *True Fan Desert Sludge with Tasty Tubers* . . .

"It's ready," said Jared, upon removing the lid of that inaugural batch.

"It's beautiful," said Clint.

"What do we call it?" asked Jared.

"It's sludge, for the True Fans."

Ahh . . . "True Fan Sludge."

17

After escaping Amboy, we were anxious to get back to civilization. But not just for the company, the air conditioning, and the cold drinks . . . Game 3 of the finals was on, and it was high time for a Jazz win.

We had all day to find a television to catch the game. The problem was, we were still in the middle of nowhere. Clint was pulling over every hundred feet to find the pregame chatter on his mini radio, purchased specifically for such predicaments on the trip. No luck.

An hour later we stumbled upon a spartan housing development, an island of civilization in the desert. We ditched the bikes and went door-to-door, asking to watch the game.

"It'll be great! They'll invite us in; we'll eat popcorn! We'll be one of the family!"

But nobody seemed too interested in hosting their long-lost sons—nobody save for one fellow who gave us the half-time score and slammed the door in our faces.

We saw the town of Cal-Nev-Ari on the map and prayed that here, there might be something.

There was.

A casino loaded with Jazz fans and the game was on every TV! To this day I've never seen Clint grin so wide as when he burst in the door. "You're just in time for the fourth quarter!" bellowed the casino-faithful.

"Thank goodness."

"You guys Jazz fans?"

Please.

"Well, they're gonna win it this year."

"Oh yeah?"

"That's what the mafia wants."

The Jazz won the game and the casino went into hysterics.

We planned to camp in Searchlight, five miles away. Searchlight is aptly named, sitting on a hill above the valley along Highway 95, "the back door to Vegas." We rolled in around ten o'clock and sniffed out the town park.

"There is only one thing that defines a great court," said Clint a few minutes later as we shot around on a near-perfect hoop in the near-perfect desert air.

"What's that, Clint?"

"The only thing that defines a great court is if you can *lose* yourself on it." Clint and I had been discussing this philosophy since high school. "You know what I mean? You can have a really nice rim and a nice net and a nice surface, but if you can't lose yourself on it, it's not a great hoop." The chain net swish-clanged.

"But if you nail a milk crate to a telephone pole in the projects and you can lose yourself on that court," Clint continued, "then that's the court I want to play on."

"Kinda like a girl," I said. "She might have the glass backboard, the breakaway rim, the polished hardwood, but if you can't lose yourself in her presence—"

"Give me the milk crate."

"Good grief," said Jared.

In the middle of the night we collapsed on the court, lying on the cement like you'd lay your head on the lap of the woman you love. We stared up at the moon beyond the trees. The dry desert breeze cooled the sweat to our backs. We were lost to the court and lost to the road at the same time. *Pilgrim's Nirvana.* All of us fell asleep right there, and slept soundly—until the sprinklers came on an hour later.

The next morning we were awakened by a strange sound. We opened the tent flap to see Richard Bennett, park caretaker, on his knees with his face against the ground, two inches from a tiny screwdriver with which he was trying to loosen nearly microscopic screws and fix one of the sprinklers we'd broken the night before.

"It is a sin, an absolute *sin* to water a court," ranted Clint when the water had come on the night before. I'd tried to push one of the sprinklers back down into the ground and had broken the head right off. This was our first battle with the sprinklers; it wouldn't be our last. In the end we'd thrown a garbage can over one, bungeed a couple more, and stuck the Sludge pot over the last one. Then we'd crawled into the tent to avoid further drenching. In all, I think there were two casualties.

But Richard never said a thing, just quietly fixed the sprinkler, offering a "Good morning!" with the cheeriest smile in the world when we shamefully exited the tent. "You guys probably gotta unload. I'll open the bathrooms right up."

"If this guy doesn't sign the Ball, then nobody's signing the Ball," said Clint as we brushed our teeth.

"You guys sleep OK?" he asked us a little later, after he'd fixed the sprinklers and refilled the garbage can we'd emptied.

"Fine."

"Well, that's what I expect to hear. This is the softest grass anywhere, you know." Richard seemed extra-special happy this glorious June day in the desert, and we asked him why.

"Well, that's 'cause I just got married."

"Really?"

"Yup. I've been a married man less than twenty-four hours."

"Where did you get married?"

But we really didn't need to ask. Las Vegas was only a day's ride away.

18

Pilgrim's Nirvana is the great gift of the pilgrimage. It is akin to being in *The Zone*, that transcendent state when the point guard cannot miss, the quarterback cannot overthrow, and every serve goes smoking down the middle of the court for an ace. How does one get into the zone? Nobody really knows.

Pilgrim's Nirvana happens like that. It comes unexpectedly: in a flash, in an instant, the pilgrim is lost to the road. What does it mean to be lost to the road? It means the world has no hold upon you. No physical hold, because you are everywhere and nowhere; no spiritual hold, because your identity is no longer bound by comparisons; rather, it crystallizes into a perfect, incomparable Truth.

You are free. You are in the zone.

You are free to do whatever you want, and the competition is powerless to stop you. You have become something greater than a good ball player; you have reached a higher plane. You have become a deity. Omnipotent? Not quite. Is it any coincidence that there are *three* refs for NBA games? For who were greater even than the gods of Olympus? The three fates that spun their destinies . . .

Freedom is the essence of Pilgrim's Nirvana as well. You are unbound by expectations, by administrations, by crippling social constructs.

You are free to be—uncategorized by comparative measures. And there are no fates—or refs—to call a double dribble. The road is your clean slate. You mark on it whatever you wish, no matter the past, no matter the future. The present expands into the gigantic, the all-encompassing, the supreme. You are free to embrace a Heroic Identity you may have only sensed before.

When the pilgrim is lost to the road, hours may pass as minutes, minutes as hours. And that elusive timelessness of childhood washes over you like sunlight through an orchard. To be perfectly at peace with where you are in the world, where you are in life—this is Pilgrim's Nirvana. Not easily acquired outside the scope of a pilgrimage, and never forced.

The zone doesn't last. No player steps onto the court every night unable to miss—even Clint. No pilgrim wakes up every morning absorbed in that glorious sense of Identity. It is a gift. But the potential remains, waiting to be unleashed when needed most, when expected least.

You can understand why that night lounging on the court in Searchlight was magical: we were spirited away twice, once by the court and once by the road.

"And when that happens," surmised Jared, "any hoop becomes the Perfect Hoop."

We could have laid on that concrete for ages.

19

"Ahh, for heaven's sake, stop. *Stop!* Can't you see we're dying out here?"

"Here comes another one, Clint."

The massive RV, loaded, undoubtedly, with every cold drink known to man, bore down on us through the heat waves.

Clint stared at the RV and its anonymous driver with an intense, desperate longing. "C'mon, c'mon! You got cold drinks; we're dying— dying!" He crossed into the lane, the RV swerved.

"Why?" he lamented as it left him behind in a cloud of dust. "Why?"

Jared and I watched this little drama for some time. "Clint, they're not going to stop," said Jared finally.

"Let it go, Clint."

"You know every single one of those things has a fridge that's loaded with Coke and PowerAde and apple juice . . ."

"We know that, Clint."

Clint shook his head and sat down on the white line. "I have never wanted a cold drink more in my entire life," he said.

Clint has a tendency to get obsessive. The day before we left Provo, our downstairs neighbor Joanna invited us over for some rich, chocolaty English sheet cake. We've already seen that Clint is powerless in the face of chocolate. He was smitten with Joanna, and would not stop talking about her the whole trip.

"Just once I'd like to see them stop."

Clint's mania wasn't so much brought on by the fact that he wanted a drink (which he really did), or the fact that it was an oven out there, but by the fact that Dammit, we deserved it—and nobody seemed to care.

"You work for every inch and you get a chip on your shoulder," reasoned Jared. This is probably why we decided not to pay camp fees either.

"Why should we pay?" Clint mused. "We don't make messes, don't use the hookups, don't make noise, don't pollute the air, don't dump twenty-five gallons of crud into the ground."

We developed something back at Big Bear called the True Fan Discount. This basically constituted paying a dollar for the camp fee instead of the outrageous fifteen or seventeen. Some places offered discounts to pilgrims—five bucks, seven bucks. That was fine. We'd probably pay that. But where there was no equity, where pilgrims were paying the same as tourists, we had to take matters into our own hands. Sometimes we felt bad about it, a prick of conscience as it were, and in these cases we repaid the government by picking up trash along the way, pulling burned-up tire husks out of the road, tossing rocks off to the side . . . We became a sort of cross-country chain gang.

Another RV was approaching, and Clint leapt up, staring down the freeway. This was a weird place we found ourselves in, a scaly, salt flat valley where prepubescent tornadoes ran amuck.

"The Tornado Academy," I said.

There were hundreds of cadets, whirling all over the flats, picking up bits of sagebrush and Snickers wrappers and chucking them around. They were feisty little tikes, the larger ones hefting sand and gravel, beer cans, water bottles, and whatever else they could get their mitts on.

When an RV came along, these brave whirlwinds would launch themselves into the middle of the road, nail the RV broadside, give it a shake, and skip off to the other side of the road, triumphant. They seemed to have minds of their own, like they were all smacking their lips over there on the flats, waiting for the next sucker to drive by.

"You take this one, Vin."

"No, no, you got it."

"It's a Holiday Rambler Imperial with roof-mounted dual trumpet air horns—"

"I hate Imperials."

"But if you could knock an Imperial off the highway . . ."

"Money."

"Big time, baby, big time."

The RV was getting closer, and Clint was launching into his mind-over-machine soliloquy: "That's right, you know we're thirsty, pull over, you'll feel so good about yourself, and you *want* to feel good about yourself, especially considering all the retirement money you're going to blow this weekend . . ."

As Clint jabbered on, Jared and I watched as one of the larger cadets made its move: it went after that RV like a defensive end after the tackle. As it hurtled across the flats it lifted its snout to the mother cloud—as if in prayer. The mother cloud reached down, the two fused together and the tornado went from chop to puree in an instant! It hurdled the embankment, whirled across the lane, and hit the RV with all it had.

Clint froze for a moment. It was like he had willed it. He stared gape-jawed as the RV shuddered over to the opposite lane and a sagebrush limb whacked it across the windshield.

But it was still too big. The cadet collapsed on the other side of the road and gasped out its last before dissolving into a spiral in the sand.

"Now that was some effort," said Jare.

The RV blew by doing ninety. It was getting the heck out of here; it wanted nothing more to do with this tornado mafia.

"Well, I feel vindicated," said Clint. "Let's go."

Three months later that same whirlwind was a first-round draft pick, picked up by some big cloud back east, and paid big money to thrash Iowa corn. His salt-flat homeys still drop in to visit sometimes on storm nights, like Allen Iverson's posse sitting courtside for the Philly games.

20

A vigorous dash of rain welcomed us to Sin City. "I've never seen it rain like this in Vegas before," said a homeless man huddled under the roof of a strip mall, playing a handheld, electronic blackjack game.

We took the rain as a good omen, and as pilgrims, made a beeline to the most appropriate hotel in town—the Excalibur. And here, because we really didn't want to miss any of Game 4, and because we needed a break from biking, and because we were dying for air conditioning, we had our one and only bona fide splurge of the trip: We got a forty-dollar room. It blew our budget to smithereens, but it did feel nice, wheeling our bikes through the casino because we *belonged*.

We locked the bikes in our twentieth-floor sardine box and headed down for the Round Table Buffet. Having just crossed the Mojave, the sight of all that limitless food was more than we could handle. We tried to be judicious, but halfway down the line the preservation instinct kicked in and it was a free-for-all.

When we got to our table, Clint had an enormous pile of food. Jared's pile of casseroles and meat was twice the size of Clint's. And my pile was twice the size of Jared's—a monstrosity.

"Are you really gonna eat all that?" Clint asked me.

"No problem. You know how much I eat."

"You can't eat all that."

"Watch me."

It was like trying to dent Devil's Tower with a teaspoon. The more I ate, the bigger the pile became. Had Merlin bewitched our portions? Across the table Clint was actually making headway. Jared, however, was in my boat and wasn't getting anywhere. And all the casserole and syrupy fruit and mayonnaise potatoes and grease were getting mixed up, forming a gelatinous mess resembling the creature in a bad '60s sci-fi movie that astronauts bring back from the moon which, despite their efforts to destroy it, just keeps growing.

Jared and I looked up from our buffet mayhem.

"I think I'm going to puke."

"Puke? You guys . . ."

"You know, Jare, I've learned my lesson. It's time for forgiveness."

"You can't just dump it out!" said Clint.

"Look at it! It's disgusting!"

"You took that food, you gotta eat it!"

"Clint, I tell you, I have learned my lesson and now I am pleading for forgiveness."

Jared agreed. "I want forgiveness too."

"Do you realize how much food you're going to waste?"

"I honestly don't think you can call this food."

Before Clint could talk us out of it, Jared and I got up, lugged our food over to the plate dumper bin, and threw everything inside. Clint was disgusted. "I've lost all respect for you guys."

"Jare, I feel so much better."

"Me too."

"How about some dessert?"

That night Clint and I biked out to the Sunset Park courts, the place to play in Sin City, or so we'd been told. It was a warm night, just the right temperature, and the courts were packed. The lights were on, and adding to the ambience, jets roared overhead on their way to land at McCarran.

We got into a couple games and played pretty well, taking off around eleven.

All through high school when we'd cruised around Cache Valley, we had a tradition where we'd stop somewhere, hop out, look around, and one of us would say: "This could be Paris," or "This could be Kathmandu." And we'd just stand there, soaking up the quiet tenor of the place until we honestly believed that wherever we were, was wherever we said.

Halfway back to the hotel we pulled over on the side of the road. We were in that empty swath of no-man's-land beside the airport. In the distance, the strip's strange assortment of shapes glowed against the sky. We rested on our handlebars and soaked up the desert night.

"You know, Clint, this could be Las Vegas," I said.

Clint just smiled and nodded.

Sure, there were more exotic places we'd visit than Las Vegas in years to come, but we were here on a pilgrimage, our Key Journey, the one that would define and empower the rest. And suddenly, all those nights of dreaming during high school back in Utah were connected. And suddenly, every time we'd said: "This could be Anchorage," or "This could be Angkor Wat," came true.

The Jazz won Game 4. Inspired by our surroundings, and the Jazz win, Clint concocted a complicated algorithm with which he could bet on sports and, if he unemotionally followed the numbers, always win.

"I really think I could do it, Dan; I think it would work." He showed me the equations after the game. "I could be a millionaire in five years."

"Are you sure?"

"Oh, I've run these numbers a thousand times. I know it seems hard to believe, but the key is just sticking to your strategy and—" Something seemed to come over him.

"What's wrong, Clint?"

"Oh, I just . . . uh . . . wait a second—" He whipped out his pocket Casio, crunched some numbers, and stared incredulously at the screen. "I think I made a mistake."

"Really."

"Seems the returns wouldn't be quite as astronomical as I expected."

"Well, how much *would* you make? Hundred thousand? Fifty?"

"After five years . . . about four hundred bucks."

"No free lunches, man."

"Guess not."

21

When you look at the pools and palm trees of Las Vegas, you naturally wonder, Where is all this water coming from? Every self-respecting casino has at least one fountain and a handful of Olympic-sized swimming pools. Las Vegas doesn't have any substantial rivers, and it doesn't rain much there. The answer, of course, is Lake Mead, a massive reservoir on the Colorado River thirty miles away, formed by Hoover Dam. Jared and I recalled a visit to the dam on our way to LA, twelve years before. Still considered an engineering marvel, Hoover Dam was the largest in the world at the time of its completion in 1935. Walls 660 feet thick at the base hold back a wall of water 700 feet high and nearly 100 miles long, an Atlasian task. Construction of the dam fomented a wave of immigration to the area. Without Lake Mead, there would be no Mirage, no MGM Grand, no Bellagio Fountains. Without Lake Mead, Las Vegas would be just another hot, dusty stop on the way to LA.

We made our escape the day after the game. Our tires felt like they were coated in molasses; three days of bad food and stale air had thrown our groove. And we hadn't spent a cent gambling. Sin City was annoyed, and was doing everything it could to keep us there. We climbed above the city and saw the deep blue waters of Las Vegas's generous benefactor in the distance, lounging among the scorched hills of Black Canyon. It was a spectacular oddity, stunning and distinctly out of place.

We rolled down into Callville Bay around seven o'clock and scouted out the campground—but there was nothing but gravel. "It would be like camping on the road," said Jared. Obviously they were catering to RVs, and the fees were out of sight.

Just above the campground on a little hill was a lush, beautiful picnic area overlooking the lake. The grass was thick and soft, there was a table to write and cook dinner upon, bathrooms were a short jog away—there was even a drinking fountain. It was a four-star campsite; the only thing missing, of course, was the hoop.

We'd learned during our first two weeks on the road that if you want to avoid getting kicked out of a campsite, it is a good idea to set up camp late—after camphosts, park rangers, and suspicious locals have turned in. We were not going to camp on the gravel, so we wandered around the bay until about ten o'clock, then set up the tent on the grass and fell asleep at once.

When you're on a pilgrimage, there is a certain magic mantra that has proven essential in getting pilgrims out of more jams than you would believe. It has the same mythic power as *Open sesame* or *Abracadabra*. It is: "*We rolled in real late last night.*" I will demonstrate.

The next morning we were awakened by a less-than-friendly voice. "Hello? Knock, knock—anybody home? Anybody speak English here?" It was a woman's voice, but not your mother's or mine.

"Morning," said Clint.

"Do you guys realize you're camping in a picnic area?"

"A picnic area? Uh, *we rolled in real late last night.*" See how useful it is?

"Well, you've got to get this tent up and move out. This is not a campground."

She walked away. It was too early; we'd been fighting the damn sprinklers all night long, moving garbage cans on top of them, wrapping bungee cords around their spindly sprinkler necks. We heard her truck rumble away and figured we were good for another hour. Not so.

Five minutes later another truck rolled up. We listened as the driver's door opened and closed, as footsteps plodded up the sidewalk. It sounded like the Marines.

I peeked out in time to see a wrinkled old guy in a brown uniform marching up the walk. Things had suddenly gone from good to crappy.

"It's the camphost," I whispered.

If there was one person to be feared in a campground, it was the camphost. These wily old folks are determined *not* to be hornswoggled out of a single penny. They take their jobs seriously, as a matter of life and death. They cannot be placated with True Fan Sludge—and they couldn't care less if you rolled in at four in the morning.

The camphost sat down on a picnic table six feet from the entrance of the tent. He just sat there for a while relishing this moment of justice. He might have been the triumphant Javert cornering Jean Valjean.

Finally, in a tone of dismay, pity, and pleasure, he said: "Looks like you boys are in a bit of trouble."

I stuck my head out. "Well, good morning, sir."

"Not for you it isn't."

"What's the problem?"

"The problem is that you're camping in a picnic area."

I looked around. "Yeah, I guess you're right."

"There are signs all over the place that say *no camping*."

"Well, that may be, but *we rolled in real late last night*."

"Don't matter; the signs are lit up."

"We had a big day, *we rolled in late*."

"And it's like anybody's going to expect us to camp on that gravel crap you got down there," said Jared, poking his head out too. "There's not a speck of grass to set up a tent."

The camphost turned toward Jared, his incredulous eyes blazing with indignation. Jared had just done the unpardonable: he had ripped on the camphost's campground.

"Well, I'll at least do my part," he said, filling out a fee envelope. "That'll be twenty bucks."

"Twenty bucks!"

"For what?"

"For camping."

"But I thought you said this was a picnic area."

"I did."

"You have to pay to use a picnic area?"

"No, just to camp in one."

"I thought you said you couldn't camp in one."

"You can't."

"Well, I guess we're off the hook."

"There is no precedent for camping in a picnic area," reasoned Jared, "therefore, since picnic areas are free-use areas, you can't legally charge us for staying here."

The camphost ground his teeth and slapped shut his little guest book, muttering, "Fine—*fine*. I tried. See now if the ranger won't have a chat with you." He stood up. "The ranger is not a nice man, not half as nice as me. He'll write you up, he'll give you all tickets—you won't know what hit you when the ranger gets done with you!"

He stomped off, ranting all the way to the truck. We counseled: "Do you think he's serious?"

"Might be."

"Could we actually get a fine?"

"Probably not, but if the ranger's anything like this guy, it might get ugly."

"Let's get outta here."

We stumbled out of the tent and started tearing things down as fast we could. The camphost saw what we were up to and yelled, "You won't get away! The ranger will be here in five minutes!" He held up a big hand, digits extended. "Five minutes!"

When he saw that we weren't listening, he got frantic. He leapt into the truck, fired up the engine, and just like that, the race was on!

We'd never taken down camp faster. We tossed everything—campstove, Sludge pot, bowls, books, bungee cords, flashlights, push-up handles—into the Ark and snapped the tarp down tight.

We threw on our panniers, threw our legs over our saddles, and hauled down the sidewalk to the road leading to the highway.

As we crawled above the bay, we saw the camphost banging furiously at the door of a house in the residential area. He turned and looked at us, staring us down with the same ghastly glare Clint had given the miserly RVs—then went right on pounding.

"I bet the ranger really hates the camphost," said Clint.

But the early departure was a blessing. A couple miles farther we saw a herd of desert bighorn standing on a hilltop. The sun was just coming up behind them, lending them a surreal backlighting; they looked like heavenly messengers. The air was cool, a welcome change, and the road was empty. We found an oasis around midday, a clear pool surrounded by palm trees. We paddled around and washed off the grime from yesterday's ride.

A few hours later we rolled into Clint's Aunt Shar and Uncle Jack's place in Overton. We watched the Jazz lose Game 6, and the finals, and I collapsed exhausted on Aunt Shar's waterbed. That was too bad, too, because we were trying to get Jared to call this girl he'd been talking about all trip and wish her a happy birthday. Had I not collapsed, I probably could have convinced him to call. Instead, six months later, she was married.

22

Like we saw above, the camphost can be a real thorn in the side of the pilgrim. You can understand their rancor. Here they are in the golden years of their lives, destined to roam Loop A and Loop B like the mythical Minotaur.

When we rolled in after dark to a campground, we'd go into *stealth mode*, saying not a word and riding along as silently as we could. If the camphost caught us, it could mean a whole day's rations down the tubes. That's a frightening thought when you consider that the only thing keeping us going sometimes was the vision of our next Frosty at Wendy's.

Usually, by uttering the holy mantra (*We rolled in real late last night*), by going into stealth mode, by using the True Fan Discount, and pinning our PAID fee stub on the post—like the mark against the destroying angel—the camphost would pass us by and we wouldn't have any problems.

Another real terror for the pilgrim is the sprinkler. Clint warned us as we began our trek that they would be formidable foes. Jared and I didn't believe it. What could be so terrifying about sprinklers? But from that first battle in Searchlight, sprinklers had risen right to the top of our True Fan shit list. The problem is detection. Even if we scouted out the area the night before and located all possible guerrillas, we were bound to miss a couple, especially if we *did* roll in real late . . . And then we'd be sleeping soundly in our tent when suddenly that horrible *cha cha cha* would rip the silent fabric of the night to pieces.

There are many different types of sprinklers. During our journey we had been putting together a sort of Audubon classification system. First, there are *Classic Rainbirds.* These are the types that everybody has in their yard, real popular in the '70s. They're distinguished by a distinct, chicken-shaped head and a trademark *cha cha cha.* Classic Rainbirds are the most easily disarmed of all the sprinklers. By simply wrapping a bungee cord around their neck or sticking a piece of wood between the kick bar and the water stream, the sprinkler will shoot off all night long in one direction.

Mushrooms are equally innocuous. They're large, black, and round and sit flush with the grass. Usually they're detectable, even at night. Like the Classic Rainbirds, they are easily disarmed with a bungee cord.

RoboHeads are a different story. RoboHeads are virtually undetectable because they too sit flush with the ground, but are much smaller than Mushrooms. In the middle of the night they pop up, casting a bead of water hundreds of feet through the air. The water shoots out so fast it can slice through the Yellow Pages.

RoboHeads cannot be disarmed with bungee cords. In Searchlight we tried to stick the Sludge pot on one, but it just blew the pot right off. Jared piled all the leftover Sludge fixin's on top of the pot to hold it down, but even that wasn't enough. We were able to take care of one RoboHead with a steel garbage can, the atomic bomb of sprinkler defense (even the most powerful RoboHead can't push over a 50-pound steel drum), but alas, there was still one left, and it was soaking the tent!

Clint never joined us for these nocturnal battles. I suppose he figured we'd get it all taken care of and that meant more sleep for him. Jared was always the first one out of the tent. More than any of us, Jared hates for his beauty sleep to be interrupted, and those damn sprinklers were going to pay. One morning in Nevada a park caretaker joked that she'd been tempted to turn on all the sprinklers full tilt last night while we lay under the stars. She thought this was funny. None of us were laughing.

So sprinklers were serious business. We ended up disarming that last RoboHead in Searchlight by taking a couple tent stakes, pounding them into the ground on either side of the sprinkler, putting the Sludge pot over the top, and clamping it down with bungee cords anchored to the stakes. It was brilliant.

"Jared, we are truly the greatest sprinkler saboteurs to ever bike across America!"

Three hours later the next round came on and we had to do it all over again. You just can't win with sprinklers.

"There's too many of them!" moaned Jared one night in Kersey, Colorado, when a whole new set we hadn't even known existed drenched everything in sight.

"I told you sprinklers were going to be a pain," said Clint, after we crawled, soaked, back into the tent.

One morning we were awakened by a whole company of Robo-Heads. We were sleeping on fresh sod in Buena Vista, Colorado. It was like an air raid. While Jared and I stumbled around in a daze, screaming directions at each other, Clint reached out from his sleeping bag and cupped his palm over a nearby offender. That was the extent of his sprinkler sabotage.

By the end of the trip, Jared and I had turned into the special ops of sprinkler disarmament. We could take out a whole park in three minutes, securing tent, bikes, and gear without getting so much as a drop on ourselves.

The things you learn as a pilgrim.

23

Much has been written of the value of water in the desert. "I've seen the time I'd drink from a muddy hoofprint," says Glen Campbell in *True Grit*. Water in the desert is the ultimate gift. In Mesquite, a day outside Overton, we camped on a grassy hill overlooking a baseball park and marveled at how the Virgin River, a mere trickle, animated the whole valley. Surely the Little Leaguers down below were grateful every summer's night for the gift. Las Vegas would be helpless without Lake Mead. The population of Eastern Africa has been clustered tightly along the Nile River for thousands of years. Nowhere on earth is water more valuable, coveted, and beautiful than in the desert.

A few years before our trip across America, I was struggling across the west desert of Colorado on my first solo pilgrimage. My bike was falling apart. The gears were grinding against the side of the frame. It was like biking through sand. And to make matters worse, I had two massive, pus-spewing rashes right up in my crotch. I hadn't noticed it at first, but the saddle had bumps on either side. After three miles of riding, it's not a big deal. After three hundred, it's a problem. On top of the rashes, I was dehydrated, I had mild heat exhaustion, and I'd been eaten alive by mosquitoes every night since Denver.

The desert is not a place you want to find yourself in such straits. I still had two days to go before I met my dad in Dutch John, Utah.

I dredged silty water out of the last available stream. I ate the last of my food. There were no cars, no shade, not even a kind cloud to diffuse the sun's rays.

Then like a mirage, an old billboard announcing the life-preserving effects of the Brown's Park Store appeared in the distance. I started celebrating—then read that it was still thirty-six miles away.

In the late afternoon, exhausted and delirious, I finally rolled up the dirt drive. Inside the converted trailer house, I babbled nonsense to the woman at the counter. "I've been on the road for a week, no, four days, and I didn't think there was a store out here—no, five days—and then I saw your sign—I had this water purifier but there's no water—the sign said thirty-six miles—I had no water—even though I had the purifier—my gears were grinding—I got these rashes in my crotch—I thought I got it fixed but they've been grinding—not the rashes, the gears—but the rashes are grinding too—I got some oil in town—this air conditioning's nice—I love air conditioning . . ."

She just stared at me.

I walked up and down the aisles for fifteen minutes, babbling, trying to figure out what to get. Need liquid. Need food. I bought a six-pack of Coke and a can of SpaghettiOs—and I didn't even have a can opener. As I rode away, I lost my balance; cradling the six-pack, I smashed against the ground. The cans ruptured. Pinned beneath my bike, I wallowed in the dirt with my lips pressed to the cans of Coke trying to suck up every drop while the precious cola sprayed everywhere.

The only shade around was the Brown's Park Store sign. I collapsed and tried to figure out what to do next. I guess somebody else knew the value of a little water in the desert and pulled over to inform me that the Green River was just a couple miles off the road, and there was a great place to swim. In my delirium, I had forgotten about the river! I bolted down the road, dumped my bike, and launched myself into the water.

The Green River in Brown's Park is wide, deep, and cold. It oozes past the parched hills, bringing life to millions of mighty cottonwoods all the way to Lake Powell. I spent the rest of the afternoon soaking in the river, watching cottonwood blossoms drift by. I hadn't loved water so much since the fountain in Ames.

Three days after leaving the baseball field in Mesquite, we were pedaling up a mild grade outside Zion National Park. At the top we saw a car, exhausted on the shoulder. Two teenagers and their mom stared at the engine. We pulled over. "You're the first people to stop," they said. "We've been sitting here for half an hour."

"What's the trouble?"

"It's seized up, vapor-locked. All it needs is a little water." We didn't have any extra and the day was hot, but we gave them all we could, about half of a water bottle. I was shocked by their gratitude. "Thank you so much! You really don't need to do this—there's not another place to get water for miles."

"I just wish we could give you more."

They were on their way to visit friends in Tropic. As hot as it was, I was surprised there weren't stranded motorists all over the place.

"How ironic," said Jared as we pedaled away. "All they needed was a little water, and it takes three bikers—three people who need it the most—to give it to them."

We came over the rise and sailed down into a wide valley, where the sunburned rock of Zion prodded up over the distant hills.

A car was coming so we pulled into a line. It was the kids and their mom; that half of a water bottle had done the trick! Their little car made the most grateful honk as they passed us, and everyone waved. How valuable is even half of a water bottle in the desert? Immeasurably so.

The day was getting hotter. Jared and I were in a serious chat about infectious disease, and Clint was up ahead working on his sunburn. At the beginning of the trip he had declared that he was going to have the best sunburn in the country, like it was some sort of accomplishment.

And man, was he nailing it—his back looked like those photos the Mars rover was sending back.

As we cruised along a car passed us from the opposite direction. None of us noticed, but the car turned around behind us, passed us again, and pulled over onto the shoulder one hundred yards in front of us. Then the window went down and three cold, sweating POWERades emerged. It was the Mom and kids. We pulled up to them; they didn't say a thing. They must have backtracked fifteen miles. We took the POWERades, thanked them profusely, especially Clint, and they were gone. Unfortunately, we didn't have time to ask them to sign the Ball.

24

Tucked away in the red rock canyons of Southern Utah, tiny creeks gouge their way through the winding turrets. Deep within these canyons, places where no trails lead, plunge hidden waterfalls into glassy-deep pools. Stand on a high ledge above these pools, take a deep, hot breath, then let the ground go for a bit and shock yourself into reality when you hit that glacier-cold water. You can see the bottom but you'll never touch it—no, not in a hundred leaps from the fifty-foot ledge.

Look across the rippling tableland from the summit above Escalante on Highway 12 and all you see is an eternity of tumble-rock, an ancient sea in flux, in the middle of its thousand-year storm. Could there be a single drop of water in that wilderness of heat? More than a drop, more than you'd ever dream. Pools nestled in shadow where tadpoles mix by the thousands in a world-beginning frenzy. Pools nestled in sinkholes, filled by rainwater from days past. Water in hiding, refugee water, running for its life through the narrow slot canyons.

Down where the walls rise like chopping blocks from the scorched sand, cottonwoods, willows, and an abundance of brush gather to hide their nurturer. But if you follow the canyon far enough, the stream may forsake its riparian shield and throw itself off a limestone cliff for a moment of liberation.

One of these streams is the impossibly chilly Calf Creek. To this day the locals wonder why the water's so cold, for it flows over bare slickrock in the desert sun. At the height of the canyon, the greatest waterfall in the red rock country leaps 126 feet off a cliff into its emerald pool. The falls have carved out an immense cathedral glowing with mosses and algae. In the summer it is an epic swimming hole, filled with mud-flinging kids sliding off the limestone walls; in the winter, the chamber grows a beard of green stalactites, dusted with snow.

And there are a thousand more hidden miracles like this, scattered far and wide across a country that at first look, appears as dry as can be.

But that's the way the desert prefers it; it likes its little secrets.

In the slots of Southern Utah every canyon has at least a little water. Not every slot trains a champion like Calf Creek Falls, but it's got something. Every drop of water from the plateau around filters down into these canyons, parenting groves, carving out streambeds. You may even get lucky and find a marsh where tasty "tubers" make a welcome addition to any Sludge.

"Just dig 'em out of the bog, chop 'em up like Rolos, and pop 'em in the Sludge," said my brother Micah on a backpacking trip through the desert a few years later. "They'll be soft and chewy in ten minutes." An hour later, they still tasted like industrial plastic.

Rising five thousand feet above the slot canyon country of pools, falls, and hidden groves, is Boulder Mountain, a veritable sprinkler head amidst the surrounding desert, appropriately named the Aquarius Plateau. If you don't look back as you ascend into the aspens, past innumerable springs and rivulets, you might forget there's a million miles of desert lapping at the feet of the mountain, scheming to leap up one day and turn it to stone. The town of Boulder sits at its base, the last town in the continental United States to receive its mail by mule.

We camped high on Boulder Mountain beside a stream. It was a different world up here, cool and peaceful, a surreal heaven floating above the furnace below. Gangs of Harley riders passed us in the morning light—it was a comforting sound, the sound of pilgrimage.

Three days later we rolled into Colorado.

25

There's a little tradition among locals to hyperbolize the unconquerable qualities of their native geographical features. I call it the "Be Scared" phenomenon. A bike shop repair guy in Sun Valley, Idaho (who should've known better), only stared at us in shock when we told him during our Jack and Dan's Tavern trip that we were going over Galena Pass. "Oh, fellas," he said, laughing hysterically, "Galena . . . are you kidding? It's *at least* twelve thousand feet"—try 8,700—"and it's gonna take you, like, *all freaking day* to get to the top—if you get up at all." Then he and his pal just looked at each other and chuckled like, *You have no idea what you're getting yourselves into.*

We were up and over Galena in about two hours, and, as usual, we took our time. But this sort of pride is refreshing, even welcome, especially when the locals actually have something to brag about. This was certainly the case when we decided to take on Engineer Pass.

Engineer Pass sits between the towns of Ouray and Lake City and accesses the sort of ethereal beauty for which Colorado is praised. Getting to Engineer Pass is glorious as well. Our first couple days in Colorado took us through the towns of Naturita and Norwood. We biked through wide-open fields where El Diente, a massive, solitary, conical peak (a *Croagh*, as the Irish would call it) loomed over everything in the distance.

Just beyond Norwood we saw a sign warning everybody of Norwood Hill. "Aw, look, guys, they named their little hill—how cute." Then suddenly the land opened up in a deep, zippered seam and we plunged a thousand feet into the heart of it. The canyon was carved out by the San Miguel River, and we camped that night on its banks.

The next day we climbed and climbed, immensely enjoying the cool air, the happy tourists, the mild-mannered Coloradoans. We passed through Ouray, where more than a few people raised their eyebrows when we told them we were going over Engineer Pass. A massage therapist invited us over to her apartment for a day's end rubdown, and we told her we were going over Engineer. "No you're not," she said.

"No, actually we are."

"You won't make it. Not with that trailer—"

"The *Ark*, thank you very much."

"Not with the *Ark*, and all that gear. It's too steep, too high, too rocky. You won't make it." This was a first. We'd been warned before, we'd been infused with fear before, our athletic abilities had been insulted before, but never before had we been told that we just couldn't make it.

"I wouldn't even try it. Go down through Durango or something."

Not only was she insulting but she gave us the creeps, and we were so anxious to leave I forgot to charge our one camera battery. This was bad news because there would undoubtedly be good material going up.

We camped at a turnout on the dirt road after about a mile. The mountain rose at a 90-degree angle on one side of the road and fell straight down to the river on the other side. We had no choice. Clint built a rock wall between the turnout and the road to protect us from wild Jeepers throughout the night. Jared made a fine Sludge to power us up the next day.

In the morning, we began the ascent.

Engineer Pass tops out at 12,800 feet, straddling a mountainous panorama strewn with abandoned mines and trestles. If lined up end to end, the mineshafts Swiss-cheesing the hills in the Ouray/Telluride area would stretch all the way to Las Vegas.

We rode across ancient bridges spanning thousand-foot chasms, dunked our heads in snowmelt as it splashed down granite shafts, and pushed our bikes up the rocky slope all day long. It got so tough that Jared, with his strongest legs pound-for-pound in America, would grind up ahead, drop his bike, and run back to push the Ark and help me.

The higher we climbed, the more spectacular it became. We passed through sparkling meadows perched on high, flat cirques, drowned with water and lit up in the sun. Some years, Engineer Pass is ice-clogged until mid-July.

The sun dipped low, then disappeared over the mountains. We were up around twelve thousand feet and suddenly it was cold. We found a hollow in the tundra, set up the tent, made a massive vat of Sludge, and rehearsed the day's accomplishments.

"Eight point nine miles," said Clint, ever the statistician. "Not even a mile an hour."

"Good night," said Jared.

The wind roared across the tundra all night long. While eating Sludge in the tent, the battery had gone completely dead. I was praying to squeeze out one, last drop of juice on top. After a final grind through walls of ice the next morning, I popped in the battery at the summit sign and hit record. I got one shot. I used it all.

From Engineer Pass the Rockies rumbled out in every direction. A diorama pointed out the more prominent peaks, 13- and 14,000-footers everywhere we looked. While we caught our breath, a well-dressed chap walking a miniature poodle tiptoed his way over to us from his Land Rover. "Helluva climb, eh?"

After a few pictures, we plunged down the trail to Lake City. By the time we got to the bottom our brakes were smoking and we were so famished we went berserk in the grocery store, buying up everything in sight. Clint lost all control, bought a bag full of junk food, plopped down on a picnic table outside, and began to feast. He didn't get far. He was so thrilled to have something besides Sludge he didn't know where to start, so he gulped down a quart of OJ and a quart of chocolate milk within thirty seconds; two minutes later, he'd collapsed on the pavement.

He didn't move for over an hour.

That night we camped along the Lake Fork River after biking through an eternal evening that refused to graduate to dusk. The next day we swam in the Curacanti Reservoir and camped in Gunnison on another church lawn. Around three in the morning Jared and I battled sprinklers—one of the worst skirmishes of the trip. With casualties mounting, we stuck our unused helmets on two RoboHeads and employed the Searchlight Method of staking and bungeeing them to the ground.

The next morning I got an idea for a cologne line.

"Summit Cologne, guys—Summit Cologne."

"So now you have a cologne line," said Jared as we packed our gear.

"*Make your pass!*" I waited for their reaction. "Make your pass! C'mon, Summit Cologne! Make your pass, you get it? Like, you make your pass on a summit and you make your pass—"

"We get it," said Jared. "It's brilliant, really."

"What does it smell like?" said Clint.

"It's got the smell of glaciers melting—"

"What do glaciers melting smell like?"

"I don't know, but it smells like that. And a pinch of sagebrush, a little rain, and a mountain stream, and—"

"Sweat. You gotta have that tangy aroma—"

"Listen up. When we get to New York, we're gonna find Calvin Klein's headquarters and pitch him this Summit Cologne idea!"

"How do you know his headquarters are in New York?" Jared asked.

"Everything's in New York," I said.

"Not the Kremlin."

"We'll march on up there in two months' time and pitch our cologne line. You think he'll go for it, Clint?"

"Uh, sure," said Clint. "Why not? It's catchy."

"Jared?"

"Make your pass. Why not."

"Summit cologne, a new fragrance from Dan Austin."

"The *only* fragrance from Dan Austin."

Around noon the hitch on the Ark snapped—probably on account of the rough descent off Engineer. We noticed the snapped hitch about the time we pulled into the tiny town of Parlin, where the town's only full-time resident, the inimitable postmaster, storeowner, mayor, and chief justice, Chuck Glaze, offered a hand.

"Give me some a' that pantha' piss," he said, referring to the WD-40. We greased up the severed hitch, knocked it out, then Chuck engineered a new carriage bolt, which he slid back in. "You may want to get it swapped out for a new one in Denver," he said, "but it should hold till then."

Chuck seemed to me a man born one hundred years too late. He stared at airplanes like he'd never seen one before, dressed like he'd just walked off the set of a John Ford Western, and reverenced the tragic deaths of western greats. "Edward Abbey's dead and John Wayne . . . what's a man to believe in anymore?"

Chuck Glaze fixed the Ark, and signed the Ball.

26

Our next challenge was Monarch Pass. While resting up before the ascent, we ran into another gang of Harley riders. These guys were the baddest of the bad, and took a keen interest in our quest. There is always a connection between bike-bound pilgrims, whether of the motorized or muscle-powered persuasion.

"I'll tell you what pisses me off more than anything," said their leader after we'd been chatting for a while. "All the trash on top—makes a mess for everybody. If I find any assholes up there littering, you can forget about the two-hundred-dollar fine."

"Listen, you guys ever break down or have trouble, we'll be there for you," another one said. "We just love the fact that you're flying the flag."

All the way up Monarch Pass our big, bold American flag flapped from the Ark. We'd been flying it since LA, but this was the first time people really took notice. It was the third of July after all; the triumphant weekend of patriotism was upon us. We camped in Monarch Meadows and the first thing next morning, Jared whipped out his harmonica and played "The Star-Spangled Banner" half a dozen times.

"We gotta get to some little town tonight," said Clint, "see some fireworks, watch the parade, celebrate America!" Between the three of us, there was enough patriotism to light a bonfire.

But from the moment we pulled out onto busy Highway 50, something was wrong. People weren't waving and cheering anymore. They were honking—and not in celebration. Usually people could get around Jared and Clint OK, but when they got to the Ark, bobbing all over the road with the flag flapping, they slowed down. Then they yelled stuff, which at first we thought was patriotic praise for our flag, but soon learned were threatening demands for us to "get the hell off the road!"

We made it off the mountain and pulled into a café at the crossroads. Here, to our further dismay, they were charging fifty cents for an eight-ounce ice water.

"Do you always charge for ice water?"

"Only on holidays."

"All I want is a nice, little town where we can kick back and celebrate," said Clint. It was a simple enough request.

We wiped out the café's condiment supply, which was our only method of retaliation (and a good way to cut costs for the cross-country pilgrim), adding the plastic packages of relish and ketchup to a massive supply pooling in the bottom of the Ark, and took off.

Highway 285 to Buena Vista was just as bad as the one from Monarch.

"The problem," yelled Jared over the roar of the highway, "is that everyone is recreating and nobody is celebrating!" Car after car loaded with dirt bikes and Ski-Dos roared past, screaming at us to get out of their way.

"This is disgusting," Clint muttered. Always so mild-mannered, he was reaching the breaking point, and once he reaches it, it's over. Another truck dragging a trailer full of four-wheelers flew by. Somebody yelled at us to watch it.

"It's time to teach these people a lesson," he said.

And with that, Clint launched himself Gandhi-like into the middle of the lane. Within minutes he had a lineup behind him a county long—but Clint, bless his heart, would not get over. "Ten miles an hour fast enough for ya?"

Jared and I watched this display of patriotic protestation from a ways back.

"Did he snap?" Jared asked.

"He snapped," I said.

"He's gonna get himself killed."

"Yup."

We caught up to him, hoping to talk him out of this madness. "Clint, what are you doing?"

"I'm taking up my own lane. I'm in the military; I fight for this country! These people need to be celebrating—this is the Fourth of July, not a three-day weekend!"

Oh, Clint was steamed, and Jared and I realized there would be no reasoning with him today. "Well, Clint, if you die, we all die." And we joined him in the middle of the lane, slowing traffic for miles. That biker gang we'd met the day before must have taken a detour, because they blazed past us again, waving and nodding. They didn't seem to care that we'd slowed them down by a few seconds. They too were flying their American flags.

"See, they get it," said Clint. "Those guys know what day it is."

After a few miles of nonviolent protest we pulled into a gas station to buy some POWERade. By this time, we were all but numb to the honks, jeers, and yells—Clint's display had turned into about the best fun we'd had all trip! I don't know whether they mistook Jared for Clint or figured bitching at one would be as good as bitching at all, but two crusty old cowboys in a pickup skidded to a stop next to Jared, rolled down the window, and yelled, "We almost ran your ass off the road! What the hell are you doing riding down the middle of the goddam lane!"

And Jared turned on them, cool and calm as ever, and unloaded: "You know what day it is? It's the Fourth of July. You see that? That's the flag of the United States of America. We're flying that flag, so you show some goddam respect!"

The cowboys were so stunned they just sat there speechless for a moment. Then the first guy rattled off a string of obscenities and they blasted away in a cloud of dust.

Clint was euphoric. "Jare! You let them have it! Holy cow, Jare, you are my hero—that was beautiful!"

Clint praised Jared all the way to Buena Vista. I sulked. I thought it was because I'd missed the scene with my camera, but really I'd just wanted a piece of the action.

We watched the fireworks that night in Buena Vista, then crashed on the park lawn. The next morning we had another drag-'em-out brawl with the sprinklers. This is where Clint "helped" by reaching out his hand to cover up a sprinkler. In the throes of the battle Jared nearly lost it himself: "Clint! Get up and help us out! Everything's getting soaked!"

We were all, I think, a little fried from the letdown on the Fourth of July. Back home in Hyrum, the greatest hometown parade in the world had taken place, my dad had brewed five gallons of homemade root beer, there were hamburgers on the grill, and endless leaps into our little sister Puff's pool.

"But cheer up, fellas," I said. "Tomorrow we reach Uncle Gary's!"

Clint demolishes the competition at Venice Beach on our first day with his trademark baseline pivot!
Photo courtesy of Dan Austin

Jared and Micah high-five as we sail down a gorgeous, pastoral highway in the rolling rangeland of Western Montana . . . We'd met little Jordan Hargrave earlier that day.
Photo by Dan Austin

The three of us get set to take off from Uncle Gary's cabin high in the mountains of Colorado after a week of barbecued steaks, poetry, and septic tank clogging.
Photo by Uncle Gary

Perhaps it was here that Clint
and I found the Perfect Hoop
. . . Sunset over the water,
shooting around together like
we have for fifteen years . . .
Photo by Tom Aaron

Just minutes after our
own Boston hot
chocolate party here
at Boston Harbor.
*Photo courtesy of
Clint Ewell*

Jared and Micah whoop it up on top of Broadsfork Twin Peaks near Salt Lake City, Utah. One of our many "pico-pilgrimages." *Photo by Dan Austin*

Jared and I sail along through the soothing flatlands of Nebraska. After a month and a half on the road, we got pretty good at riding and shooting at the same time. *Photo by Clint Ewell*

Jared and Micah wave from a rugged dirt road in Yellowstone National Park during our journey home. *Photo by Dan Austin*

Somehow we survived the best storm of the trip in Nebraska City, Nebraska. In the morning, we draped the town park's jungle gym with our soaked gear and waited for everything to dry.
Photo courtesy of Dan Austin

Jared records one of my typical impassioned soliloquies during a break in the rain, deep in the woods of West Virginia.
Photo by Clint Ewell

A reflective Clint pulls to the edge of the pier in Asbury Park, New Jersey. For Clint, hitting the Atlantic Ocean was the high point of the trip.
Photo by Jared Austin

We found this ancient hoop near Grand Island, Nebraska. The court was filled with cracks and weeds . . . but that didn't stop Clint from shooting around.
Photo by Dan Austin

Nothing makes you feel more triumphant than conquering a summit—especially 12,800-foot Engineer Pass! Jared and I flex for the camera in front of the summit sign.
Photo by Clint Ewell

We found this shrine in Capital Reef National Park, Utah. Water is the Pilgrim's friend!
Photo by Jared Austin

Jared and I take in the National Mall in Washington, D.C. We sat on the steps of the Lincoln Memorial and pondered our trip and our great country for hours.
Photo by Clint Ewell

We met True Fan Kerry Coyne in Boston where she was a waitress working her way through school. She actually paid for all of our dinners herself—one of the most sincere acts of kindness we'd witnessed all trip.
Photo courtesy of Clint Ewell

We find ourselves lost deep in the heart of the Mojave Desert, biking through cathedrals of Joshua trees and scrub oak . . . We still have miles to go before intersecting with Route 66.
Photo by Clint Ewell

The bikes get a breather on the shores of the Mississippi River in Nauvoo, Illinois.
Photo by Clint Ewell

A great moment of Pilgrim's Nirvana: everybody kicking back on this quiet Idaho highway—the road is more comfortable than you might think. We're on our way to Jack and Dan's Tavern in Spokane, Washington. This was the beginning of our first journey together.
Photo by Dan Austin

After traveling 4,800 miles, we join our fellow True Fans from coast-to-coast as we sign the Hero's Ball.
Photo by Jared Austin

Journey's end: The Basketball Hall of Fame, in Springfield, Massachusetts.
Photo courtesy of Dan Austin

The Hero's Ball enshrined in the Basketball Hall of Fame.
Photo by Dan Austin

27

Since those early high school days, it had become a tradition to hit Uncle Gary's during a pilgrimage. As luck would have it, Uncle Gary had recently moved into a little cabin high above the Denver metro. The cabin represented the culmination of a long-standing dream of his, to extricate himself from civilization. It wasn't that Uncle Gary really disliked people—just people in large quantities.

Uncle Gary's cabin lay sequestered away in the woods near Bailey. On the sixth of July, we pulled into the Chevron at the Bailey junction to ask directions. The instant we walked in the door the woman behind the counter acted like she knew us. This was because she sort of did. "Your uncle was in here a while ago . . . Oh, he's worried sick about you guys! He hopes you make it OK."

But there was no way we weren't going to make it; the thought of a few days of relaxation, Uncle Gary's steaks on the grill, cold cream sodas—it was enough to drive a man insane. Especially Clint, who was still on edge after the Fourth of July extravaganza and seemed to think the world still owed him his own lane.

Getting to Uncle Gary's proved tricky, as the Bailey area is a mass of roads splitting off from roads, splitting off again. It seems the property got bought up in a frenzy and nobody thought too seriously about any sort of order. The result is a mad rash of cabins, chalets, abandoned trailers, and forgotten cottages strewn like glacial moraine across the hills.

After nine miles we pulled into the "town" of Harris Park—just a crisscross of dirt roads and a community center. A quarter mile up Neal Street we found the good uncle's hidden retreat. Words cannot express our joy in reaching Uncle Gary's cabin.

We knocked and Uncle Gary, wearing an XXX-Large Colorado Rockies T-shirt, flung open the door. "The X-Men are here," he said.

We got right down to business.

"Looks like you all need a shave and a shower," said Uncle Gary. We took turns releasing ourselves from three weeks of filth, then ambled out back and took a seat on the deck. Steaks were already on the grill, and Uncle Gary had stocked up on cream sodas, chips, salsa—the works. The day was breezy and quiet in Harris Park. From the deck we could see way up to "Mad Loon Ridge," as Uncle Gary called it, covered with pine forests, rising three thousand feet above us. Just below the cabin an empty lakebed lobbied for water, a sign on the "bank" telling everyone there was no fishing allowed.

"I can't believe we're here," said Jared.

"We've been looking forward to this for weeks," I said.

"Now, tell me how you survived 285 on Fourth of July weekend?"

"We nearly didn't."

"Clint almost got us killed."

"I was just exercising my freedoms," said Clint, appearing on the deck with a towel around his waist.

"When did you guys shower last?" This took a moment.

"Las Vegas," we said. Uncle Gary couldn't believe it. "I hope you don't clog the drain." The drain wouldn't be the only thing we'd clog before the end of this sojourn.

"Did you watch the finals?" we asked. Uncle Gary's face went grim, like we'd just broached a tender subject. "I will never forgive them for what they did to us."

"They?"

"The refs."

"To this day I believe the Jazz won," said Clint.

"I was so mad," Uncle Gary said, clenching his fists. "All those missed calls at the end, all those mistakes."

"Even *with* the mafia's support."

"I sat there watching Jordan and his thugs whoop it up, and I got so upset that I took off out my front door and went running up this trail I like to walk to Mad Loon Ridge as fast as I could, straight up the damn mountain. I ran and ran, I was so angry; I ran until I got to this pond about a mile up, then I collapsed and puked my guts out and bawled. I call it the trail of tears and vomit."

None of us really knew what to say after this. I mean, there are fans and there are *fans*. We were a little disheartened after the loss, but heck, it's just basketball, and there's always next year. "Well, that's, that's pretty—"

"Pathetic. I know. But you live alone like this and you start to live through other people."

With that painful catharsis off his chest, things lightened up again. "I've been working on some new poems," he said.

"Oh yeah?"

"I like sitting out here in the evenings, just like this. The words come easily."

"Let's hear one, U.G."

"This one's called 'Dreamless Slumber'—.

> *I walk the ridge to make the sunlight last,*
> *the way the morning snow had melted, fast.*
> *October is the loneliest of months, and dim*
> *blurred and secret as a canyon rim.*
> *As usual, the trees are hoarding snow,*
> *in shadow hiding what they cannot grow.*
> *The aspen branches laid out bare*
> *prove all their lives are buried there.*

My brothers, hunting, left me with the trees
they told me I could count the leaves
in that October thirty years ago,
I knew even then, what I could not know.
I knew even then October light,
seen from deep shadow, would be my last sight."

"Not bad, Uncle Gary."

"I was in the woods the other day and wrote a poem about the black squirrels."

"I've never seen a black squirrel."

"They're very wise, and I knew as I sat there against the tree that they were watching me."

"How did you figure this out?"

"Like I said, you live alone, you start to compensate for the lack of human interaction." He eased back in his chair. The evening had fallen; already the bug lamp had smoked its first few customers.

"It starts out innocently enough," he began. "You start hearing voices, voices in your head and voices from the animals. You try to ignore them, but they come at you more and more persistently until you're lying in bed at night listening quite calmly as all the deer and birds have these elaborate conversations about survival and sex—you know, the usual topics—then suddenly you find yourself screaming with the loons on Mad Loon Ridge and running on all fours through beds of pine needles, rolling in bear scat—and you're having long, one-sided conversations with squirrels that last all night, and pretty soon they become two-sided conversations . . ."

He trailed off, eyes rising to the heights of Mad Loon Ridge. "It starts out innocently enough," he finished.

The night deepened. We devoured an obscene amount of food.

"I think we need some Jacques Brel," said Uncle Gary. He put on an old vinyl and the melancholy French singer came crashing through the door with a bottle of wine in his hand. "How long have you had this record?" we asked.

"Twenty years!" he said. And suddenly we saw a younger Uncle Gary trudging through the foothills of the Pyrenees as a missionary in his hopeful youth.

"Where I thought I'd be in twenty years!"

"But you have your retreat," we said. "You are the Thoreau of these woods; you have your Walden Pond, albeit dried up."

"Yeah, that's sort of funny; the kids drive their four-wheelers through Walden every day."

Three years later, Uncle Gary and I went to Paris together. I'd always dreamed of going to Paris in the springtime with a special someone. I never dreamed it would be Uncle Gary. *True Fans* had been invited to screen at a festival in Val d'Isère, a hip French ski town in the Alps. The festival had flown me over, covering everything, including three days of skiing. I was thrilled. It was Uncle Gary's first return in nearly twenty-five years.

He arrived before me and told me when we met in Paris that he'd gone to visit Compiègne, a town up north where he'd spent a few months. As he was walking down the road a man burst out of his house, ran up to him, grabbed him by the collar on his shirt, and said, "*Je te connais! Je te connais!* (I know you!)"

"As it turned out," Uncle Gary said, "he was just a boy when I was there. We'd been friends."

"What happened?"

"We went inside and ate dinner. I met his family. He had a wife, a couple kids. Then I walked off into the woods, the woods I used to roam back then, the woods where I buried one of my wisdom teeth. I sat down in a clearing and stared up at the sky. I never would have thought twenty-five years ago that I would be coming back like this. Then the rain began to fall and I cried and cried. I fell asleep crying in the rain

and woke up shivering at four o'clock in the morning. The moon was
out. I stared at the moon and wondered where all the time had gone."

I can still see my uncle, much younger and happier, riding up in his Jeep
fifteen years ago, the world just shining. And all my actor friends hop-
ping in with the costumes I'd made, with the scripts I'd written, with all
the magic trinkets Uncle Gary had brought back from the four corners
of the world: a glass egg from Cairo, a dagger from Guatemala, a jade idol
from Venezuela . . . *Search for the Disk of Rocone, The Forbidden Crystal, The
Coming of the One-Eyed, For Fear, Curse, Vengeance*—all those first movies
made in the innocence and happiness of youth. All those wonderful,
sparkling times! Looking back, I realized I relished the journey to those
magical places to shoot the scenes just as much as I loved the process of
making the movie. The trip and film were one back then, too.

"Well, nephews," said Uncle Gary, hours later, "you must be tired."
     We were, but it felt so good to relax out back, knowing we didn't have
to battle sprinklers tonight or bike tomorrow, knowing no camphost was
going to wake us up at 6 A.M.
     "I'll see you in the morning," Uncle Gary said. A while later, Jacques
Brel's brooding voice once again lifted like a ghost through the house.
     And in his little bedroom, Uncle Gary dreamed of France.

> *The night lamps spill amber pools on the Compiègne*
> > *Bridge,*
> *like the yellow fields of rapeseed south of Paris*
> *billowing beyond the view of trains and eyes;*
> *and skies, gray as the water*
> *and the barges between Paris and the sea,*
> *that ocean greener than the Ardennes in April.*
> *The village I love is a river in France,*
> *the rivers and towns are the same to me,*

whether the Rhone or the Seine, Compiègne or Paris,
the rivers and towns flow down to the sea.
If I returned somehow to the river that was,
remembering all that I used to be,
could I see myself standing here twenty years hence
with time running down like this river in France
to the sad salt taste of eternity.

28

We spent a week at Uncle Gary's. Every day we'd ride down to Denver with him, and while he was at work at the U.S. Geological Survey, we'd check out the town. There were a few things we needed to accomplish. The frame on Clint's bike had snapped a weld back in Buena Vista, and we needed to get it replaced. I needed to buy a few more tapes, and the Ark of the Covenant needed a new hitch.

Every night we'd return to the cabin, sit out back, and watch the storm clouds skulk across Harris Park, getting all tangled up on the prickly spine of Mad Loon Ridge. Uncle Gary had an endless supply of steaks and chicken; we ate like kings, wrote like bards, recited poems long into the night, took long walks through town, around Walden, through the woods, discussing the trip and the things we'd seen.

One day we were sitting out back, and it was one of those breezy, dreamy afternoons. Uncle Gary just turned to us and quite calmly said, "Stay—stay here with me. Never leave. You should stay."

"We've got to finish the journey, Uncle Gary."

■ ■ ■

I remember the day when we all felt it was finally time to go. You always know when it's time to move on; the road will call to you. You don't need to decide a thing. You just listen.

"You've got that *thousand-mile stare* going," said Uncle Gary the night before the departure. "That's the same stare I used to get the night before I'd embark for Cairo, Caracas, Guadalajara."

Following his two years in France, Uncle Gary had traveled the world, hopscotching from one end of it to the other. He worked on an oil ship, and had all sorts of adventures, adventures that had inspired those first films. He told us stories of tribes deep in the Amazon who spoke of visitors from outer space, stories of maniacal monkeys stealing money and framing shipmates while out to sea. Uncle Gary was a modern-day Sinbad to us back then.

"Did you ever want to get married?" Clint asked him late that night as we gathered our gear.

"I had my chance," he said. "She was way out of my league . . . but I thought we had something. I really did. We met in a snowstorm at four o'clock in the morning in front of Gilgal Gardens in Salt Lake City. For some reason I spoke French to her. She spoke back. She was French. Only woman I ever kissed."

"What happened?"

"One day she said she wanted to go for a walk, so we did. We walked into this little grove. It was in the fall, and the colors were beautiful. I was happy. Then she told me—as gently as she could, I think—that it was over. I didn't think someone could hurt me so bad. I just didn't think it was possible. I'll never forget how, right after she said this, the tree behind her suddenly lost its leaves. I'll never forget that . . . nor will she, I imagine."

Uncle Gary didn't say much the next morning as we left. His face was empty and drawn, not unlike the face of the little sad man in Amboy.

He'd miss us. We'd clogged his septic tank, his shower drain, eaten him out of house and home, and used up seven rolls of TP, but he'd miss us.

"Remember, nephews, remember: next time you're staying with someone, it is common courtesy to use less toilet paper."

"Thanks for everything, Uncle Gary."

The good uncle nodded. "Have a Coke in Conifer," he said.

And we were off.

29

Before we started across America, a fellow in a bike shop had given us some advice about the plains. "Get through them as fast as you can," he'd said. "When I biked from New York to San Francisco, I woke up at six every morning, went hard till eight at night, and was through 'em in a week."

But from the moment we left the Denver metro and began the soothing, gentle descent to the Mississippi, a calm settled over us. We lost track of hours, and distance—we'd bike a mile, then realize we'd biked ten. We'd find ourselves suddenly weaving in and out of the dashes on the road in an unspoken contest of follow the leader. For all we cared, we'd *never* make it through the plains.

The plains are not the place to go for the big bang—unless you're in the middle of a storm. The plains are the place you go to think. You can't help but get introspective stepping out of your front door everyday and seeing miles and miles of farmland, hills, little forests, and languid streams. Ideas explode like thunderheads. It is a land without boundaries, borders, or limits. It beckons the wanderer and the wandering mind like nowhere else. It inspires the endless ramble. Out West a mountain may block your path, but here, nothing more impassable than a barbed-wire fence stands in your way.

■ ■ ■

The moment we hit Nebraska, everybody started waving at us. Nowhere else had people consistently waved first. Highway 30 shot out in front of us like the yellow brick road, slightly elevated over the rush of fields and sprinkler systems. The day, like every day on the plains, was sparkling hot and muggy—full of cicada song, and the *cha cha cha* of sprinklers. Despite our many battles with RoboHeads and Classic Rainbirds, we found these sprinkler titans enduringly fascinating. During the hot, hypnotic afternoons we'd find ourselves pulled off to the side of the road gazing at the dinosaurs as they drank up water and spat it out in three-hundred-foot streams across sparkling acres of thirsty green. It was all so orderly and beautiful. And this is what we loved most about the plains: it is here that the mechanics of the universe are on full display. You watch the sun rise and set, unobstructed; you see the fields soak up every ray and watch the farmers sculpt that raw sun-energy into soy and corn. You know a little piece of the sun, the earth, and the man is encapsulated in that apple you picked off a tree a mile back. Then the sun sets and the stars whirl through the sky and a harvest moon creeps up over the grain silos and the rippled hills, like a lost balloon from the county fair. Sunsets are blood-red and endless. Everyone drives slowly, as if in constant marvel of the wonder of creation.

And there's always a baseball game going on somewhere. Fly over the plains at night and that's all you see, pockets of light, baseball diamonds, where dramas unfold, where parents watch, kids check out the new kid, heroes are done and undone, legends are spoken of. It's not unlike the basketball court, and it's happening all the time.

On the plains the trains chug on endlessly, toiling away with tons and tons of coal on their backs, bound for who knows where. Hopefully not Amboy.

The day before we crossed from Colorado to Nebraska, we camped in the town of Julesburg, right on the border. Here, we got our first taste of true plains living—water tower, tidy neighborhoods, well-kept road-side park a stone's throw from the tracks.

I could not have been happier to be camping near the train tracks. Jared, however, felt otherwise. "Oh, it's great, Jare—the trains just lull you to sleep!"

Right.

The last time I camped near the tracks was three years before with the most beautiful girl on the planet. She'd moved to Oregon on a spiritual quest to find her birth mother after a passionate summer of all-night kissing and mini-pilgrimaging. A couple weeks later, unable to withstand the distance, we'd met halfway in Baker, Oregon, in the crisp fall.

Neither of us had any money, of course—it had taken all I had just to buy the gas to get up there—but oh, was I happy to see her, and we had a blast. One night we threw the family-sized elk hunter sleeping bag out on the lawn of an elementary school. The bell woke us up the next morning as all the kids ran past us to class.

Another night we camped in what I thought, in my impassioned delirium the night before, was an abandoned lot.

Late that night we were making out in the backseat when suddenly we heard a roar and felt the ground shake; we bolted upright to see a beam of brilliant white light blasting through the back window. We were both on the verge of a scream before we realized the train was going to miss us by about fifteen feet.

I looked at Melanee. Her perfect little face was bathed in the scattered, dance-club array of light cast by the passing train.

"Nice choice," she said.

Once you think you're going to die—then you don't—kissing's really nice.

So sleeping by railroad tracks held a certain affection for me, and I convinced Jared that there was nothing so soothing—save perhaps the moaning of Jacques Brel—to sing you to sleep.

"Matter of fact, let's camp as close as we can."

It was about 1 A.M. when the first train came through. We had just finished reading and writing and chatting, and were all hunkered down in our sleeping bags amid the chirping black. Suddenly, we heard that banshee cry from the far distance, then the piercing light, and then the roar—

Jared sat up fast, from dead asleep to fully awake, gasping. I can only imagine he felt the same, horrified exhilaration I had felt when, mid-make-out, I thought we were about to get bashed into oblivion.

"I hate trains," he muttered, throwing the sleeping bag over his head.

But there were at least a dozen more before dawn, and Jared jerked awake for every one. In the morning he looked like he'd just been plowed by one of the big engines.

"I hate trains. We're never sleeping next to the tracks again." Clint, of course, could sleep through a rock concert, and didn't complain.

"I'm with Dan," he said. "I too find it rather soothing."

One thing that made Jared such an effective sprinkler saboteur was the fact that he *hated* to be awakened more than anybody, and even counted up the minutes of rejuvenating REM sleep he was losing in the process of thwarting our foes. It was all a mission to him, a mission to save his sleep—and the clock was ticking.

And now trains were in the sprinkler category; just that you couldn't exactly string a bungee cord across the tracks and bounce them back the way they came.

30

Every night Jared explored new strategies for dealing with the trains: earplugs, Ibuprofen, self-hypnosis. With countless battles under his belt by the time we reached Iowa, trains were no longer a nuisance. Three years later in Scotland, however, he met his match.

This time we were camping at a place called Cape Wrath, which is the northwestern tip of Scotland. Cape Wrath looked pretty cool on the map when we planned the trip, so we decided to go. Locals along the way apprised us of what to expect: "There's nothing at Cape Wrath but wrath," growled one old Scotsman. With every adventure, locals all over the world kept proving the "Be Scared" phenomenon—their pass is always the highest, their winters always the coldest, their forests always the darkest. Incidentally, their women are always the best looking as well. It's really nice to see, this hometown patriotism. But it's usually a bunch of hogwash when you get right down to it.

Cape Wrath, like Engineer Pass, did not turn out to be hogwash.

To reach Cape Wrath, we first had to cross the spectacular, spongy, lonely Highlands; next, a ferry across an icy inlet on a leaky, old fishing boat. Then, a winding, Dr. Seuss-like road that crossed a bombing range for the Royal Air Force (and luckily, there were no signs, as there often are, saying BOMBING TODAY, NO ACCESS, PLEASE TURN AROUND—like blowing up landscapes is as innocuous as a Tupperware party). And finally, after a twelve-mile roller coaster ride through canyons and hills and mountains, arrival at the edge of a becliffed tentacle of land jutting out five hundred feet, straight up over the glimmering North Atlantic. It appeared to be the end of the world, the end of the universe, the end of everything.

Everything—except for a lighthouse.

"You know," said Jared, greatly loosened up from his trip across America three years earlier and ready to take on everything from saber-toothed tigers to Himalayan passes, "you know, we've never camped at a lighthouse before . . . We should camp *right here.*" He planted the staff of our American flag into the earth. It was a nightly ritual on our foreign trips, to claim our campsites *in the name of the United States of America!* (A ritual that would bite us hard in the rear in Northern Ireland five hundred miles later.)

But tonight this land was ours, and we all agreed that this would indeed be a prized campsite and a first in True Fan history.

Micah, who had replaced Clint on this trip, set up the tent. Then the mist rolled in off the sea, as only mist in Northern Scotland can. We crawled into our sleeping bags, and just when we were at the point of total relaxation—the distant sound of the sea, the cool air, and the soft, spongy earth coaxing us far, far away from this grim world of turning pedals day after day—right then, as Jared was logging his first few, coveted REMs—the most enormous sound I have ever heard yanked us back to consciousness with the combined force of a *fleet* of freight trains. It was, of course, the foghorn.

We're from Utah, a landlocked state. So when we think of lighthouses, we naturally think of light, not necessarily sound. That said, none of us had taken much notice of the big, horn-shaped thing near the spot where we'd parked our tents. We thought it was some sort of relic on display. In fact, it was the biggest damn foghorn in creation.

After the *OOOOMMMM* had faded away, we looked at each other, shrugged, and said, "Well, I'm glad that's over," and lay back down to go to sleep. The grass was soft, the air cool, and before we knew it, Hypnos was reaching out for us again, when—

OOOOOOOOOMMMMMM

This time, it was about ten times as loud as the first time.

"You know," said Micah, after the horn had faded, "it's really not *that* loud." Too tired to consider any alternative, we lay back down. The next time it was about ten times as loud as before. I could feel my eardrums rattling like popcorn kernels. That was when we decided, tired or not, that we should move.

The only place we could move the tents that would offer any refuge from the horn was behind a brick wall in back of the lighthouse. To relocate there, we would have to brave the sheer cliffs, now slippery with dew, which fell abruptly close by.

Delirious with fatigue, nearly blind by the mist, and ridiculously unbalanced with the tents over our heads, we tromped around the side of the lighthouse and hunkered down below the wall.

"It's still too loud," said Jared with a T-shirt wrapped around his head.

Ever the survivor, Micah had already disappeared into his sleeping bag and was halfway to dreamland when we got another surprise.

"Hallo there!"

We poked our heads out of the tent to greet two amiable Scots walking from the lighthouse over to the wall. "What in God's name are you doing here tonight, lads?" they asked.

"Camping," we said.

"Camping? Lord—on Cape Wrath?"

We nodded, wriggling back outside.

"We were up top and saw you carrying your tents through the mist—just that; all we saw were the tents—and I said, 'Holy God, what in the bloody hell is that?'"

"We came down to investigate," said his pal. "We didn't think anybody on the planet would be foolish enough to camp at Cape Wrath."

We were proud to prove them wrong. Have you ever noticed, by the way, how the heroes in mythology and literature are usually imports? That's because everybody who has to deal with the Minotaur, the Hydra, Medusa, or Smaug on a daily basis is too traumatized from a lifetime of exaggeration to do anything about it. Ignorance is not only bliss, but power.

"So, what brings you to Cape Wrath?" they asked.

We told them we were biking through the British Isles, en route to Wantage, England, the hometown of our ancestor, King Alfred the Great, the only king in medieval history to successfully repel—and even convert—the Vikings.

"Do you think you could turn that horn off for us?" Jared asked. "I've got to get some sleep." The two looked at each other, then broke into laughter nearly as potent as the horn. "Oh, lad, turn the horn off . . ." They laughed for some time.

"I take that as a no."

"Hey, Harry, why don't you go turn the mist switch off, then we won't need the horn, then these guys can get all the sleep they want!" They bellowed on and on. Jared wasn't laughing. He was too tired to find anything humorous at this point. Between the horn and these comedians, he'd already lost several thousand REMs.

"So, you guys live here?" asked Micah.

"Well, not really; we're what you call lighthouse checkers. We spend two weeks at a time at lighthouses all over Great Britain, make sure everything's working well, fix anything that isn't, and move on to the next." Lighthouse pilgrims.

"We've been doing it for years," finished his friend.

"Do you get lonely?"

"Aye, all the time; miss me family. But you get used to it."

"Now don't get too close to that cliff; we lost one a few weeks ago . . ."

"Really."

"Yeah, we lose about one a year. She was taking a picture, wasn't looking where she was stepping and *whoosh* . . . she's gone." He told the story so matter-of-factly you'd think people were falling to their deaths there every day.

And then this strange night of mist, horns, and lighthouse hermits got stranger still. Through the mist, in the direction of the road that led to Wrath, there suddenly appeared, like the apparition of Hamlet's father on the heath, a lone pilgrim with a massive pack on his back.

"What in God's name?" said the first lighthouse guy. "Another one?"

"Busy night," said the other.

"I thought you said nobody camped here."

"I did."

The visitor was a Korean pilgrim hiking down the coast of Scotland. He chatted with the lighthouse keepers for a few minutes before wisely choosing to camp a quarter mile away.

"We're gonna have to start chargin'," said the first keeper. They turned back to us and shrugged off a chill.

"Well, we've got some tea on upstairs. Have a good night," one keeper said.

"I'll work on that horn problem," his friend added. They both chuckled and the mist gobbled them up. The Korean had disappeared too.

"You know, they could turn that horn off if they wanted too," said Jared.

"Then what would the ships do, Jare? Get all smashed up on the rocks?"

"That just happens in the movies; I bet they don't even use these things anymore."

■ ■ ■

After a nightlong battle with the foghorn, we opened our tent flaps to a shining, silvery new day. It was so spectacular we forgot all about foghorns and REM sleep and just gazed out over the ocean.

Jared had ended his feud with the foghorn; I saw him over there getting a few stills to show the landlocked folks back home what to avoid if they ever pitched their tents in the land of the lighthouses.

31

Halfway across Nebraska Jared resigned himself to the fact that dealing with trains was simply a way of life. If you want grass, you have to camp in the park. Most parks are near the tracks; therefore, Mr. Train is going to be your friend, whether you like it or not.

In York, Nebraska, another menace arrived on the scene: mosquitoes. And not just any mosquitoes; these were bioengineered monsters with ten times the sucking capacity of the native species. I hadn't seen such mosquitoes since Brown's Park, five years ago during my first solo pilgrimage.

We dumped on every ounce of available repellent. We rolled around in the dirt. We lit three of those useless mosquito coils and sat motionless between them, hoping the smoke would provide a screen. It was too hot in the tent and our sleeping bags felt like chrysalises around us. Between mosquitoes and foghorns, I'd take foghorns every time.

The next day we spent the long evening hours on the steps of the capitol in Lincoln; a few nights later in Nebraska City, we braved the biggest storm of the trip. We watched it come, heard it come, *felt* it come; we were all huddled under a gazebo in the town park and figured we'd just sit there and "watch the show." Funny, to curious locals across the street, we would *become* the show.

Around 4 A.M., the biggest thundercrack we'd ever heard jerked us all awake. It was like God busting a two-by-four over his knee. Then things got nasty. Jared decided we'd better set up the tent. Clint and I, bracing ourselves against the gazebo's support beams, just stared at him, stupefied, as he tried to cram the poles through the nylon sleeves in sixty-mile-an-hour winds. I guess he figured that inside "tent world" everything would be hunky-dory. Then the rain blew in, like somebody just flipped a switch and the nearby Missouri gushed down. We heard another *crack*—it was a tree limb on the other side of the park getting ripped off like a chicken wing. A block away a twister demolished somebody's living room. We could only guess it was the talented whirl-wind we'd met earlier in Nevada, showing off his big-league contract.

This went on for about an hour. Jared finally gave up trying to set up the tent and hugged a support along with us. Lightning flared up all around us, and the thunder sounded like a 21-gun salute. Twenty-one, 21-gun salutes.

Finally, the wind abated, the thunder moved on, the lightning burned out its heavenly filaments, and we just sat there on the picnic table under the gazebo catching our breath, watching the downpour.

In the morning, massive thunderheads skulked in the distance. They looked so heavy you'd think a mile of steel cable was holding them up, like a suspension bridge. A nice old man ambled across the street. "I'm surprised to see you're still here. I figured the tornado woulda gotcha," he said.

He offered us some hot chocolate and we chatted for a bit. The morning sky was bruised and pink, the birds chirping optimistically, like they always do—like there's never a problem. We flung all our wet stuff, which was basically everything, over the playground jungle gym to dry. Jared and I took a walk to survey the damage. We found the tree limb. "I remember hearing that thing go last night," he said. "I thought, Holy crap, we're dead."

An hour later the hometown reporter stopped by to see if we were still alive—and if so, how—and to ask us a few questions about the trip. This is another great advantage of going on a pilgrimage: invariably you will get in the newspaper. Small-town folks find it fascinating to hear what you're up to. You feel like you're the first guys ever to bike across America.

"I really can't believe you guys survived the night," the reporter said. "That was the biggest storm of the summer, for sure."

We all chuckled. Here we were again, mind-boggling the locals by slaying their dragons.

The reporter promised to send us a copy of the article, laughed her silly laugh, and was gone. We spent the next three hours milling around the park, waiting for our gear to dry.

32

No matter whether you cross into Iowa from the Illinois side or the Nebraska side, the topography changes: the land turns from tabletop to rolling sea. Nothing's all that flat in Iowa. It's like the two mighty rivers between which it sits, the Missouri and the Mississippi, squeezed the land together and caused it to buckle. The result is some of the best riding, because the terrain is infinitely variable, full of hollows and nooks.

That evening we rolled into Clarinda, Iowa, hometown of Glenn Miller. The sun was sinking and it seemed everybody in town had gathered at the Cool Cats shaved-ice shack a block from the square. We pulled in to join the throng and ordered a round of snow cones.

Here we met Gary Kelley, sitting astride his Harley, with his young friend Marty by his side. Gary was a pilgrim to the core, a fifty-something roamer who had returned to Clarinda after a twenty-year absence. We immediately hit it off and he invited us over for the night.

"I grew up here," he told us. "Like a lot of kids who grow up in Iowa, I couldn't wait to leave."

By now, evening had fallen, cricket song was everywhere, and people were moseying in and out of Gary's house like it was their own.

"When I graduated from high school everybody knew I was getting out of here, and they asked me if I thought I would ever come back. I said, when I can come back in my Lear jet, I'll be back."

Marty, Gary's eighteen-year-old Harley-riding apprentice, stopped by with an armload of corn. "This is Iowa corn, the best corn in the world. I just picked it." He tossed it into a pot of boiling water.

"My goal was to be a millionaire by the time I was forty," said Gary. "And I almost made it. But then a lot of things happened all at once: I got forced out of the business I helped to build; I got divorced—talk about an asset liquidation plan," he laughed. "And the next thing you know, I don't have anything. No money, no career, no wife, no family, nada."

These sorts of stories—going from everything to nothing, and that very *nothing* realigning the pilgrim's life—were becoming commonplace. We'd hear several more before the trip was through. Perhaps it's impossible to know what you truly want, when your life is still cluttered with all the crap you *think* you want.

"What did you do?" Jared asked.

"Well, I was reading *Zen and the Art of Motorcycle Maintenance*, you know, and I was kind of intrigued by the lifestyle, so I went out and bought a 1981 Kawasaki 650 LTD. My grandma made me a pair of saddlebags, and I took off. I roamed America for four months."

"What were you looking for?"

"Don't really know," he said. "I think I was looking for something to happen . . . I don't know what. I spent some time in Missouri with my dad on the hog farm; I spent some time in New Orleans with a friend who said he could get me crewed up for a Chuck Norris picture. That never happened. Finally, I just came back home. To Clarinda."

He didn't come back in a Lear jet with a million dollars; Gary came back with empty pockets and an old motorcycle about ready to give up the ghost.

"I got involved in the community, I started working with inmates at the prison, I got elected to the city council. And one night I realized, I'm happy again."

In the five years since his return, he'd become a town father to the community, evidenced by how welcome everyone felt in his place. Gary had to leave to take care of his ninety-six-year-old grandma that night, but he gave us free rein of the house.

"If I don't see you in the morning, guys, have a great trip."

But we would see Gary Kelley in the morning. On our way out of town we stopped by the Clarinda Correctional Facility where Gary worked as a mentor. Three years later, Gary would show my film *True Fans* to its nine hundred inmates.

Gary saw us roll up and came outside to see what was going on.

We asked him to sign our Hero's Ball, of course. After signing he just stared at the Ball and all the other signatures, all the other Heroes bound for the Hall of Fame. He didn't say anything for a long time.

33

Rivers are the earth's pilgrims. They have a beginning and an end, but their journey is ceaseless.

Every pilgrimage begins and ends, and yet, in the soul of the pilgrim, those storied waters flow on forever.

God calls prophets to mountaintops; pilgrims call on God from rivers. John the Baptist knew it; the several million pilgrims who travel every year to the temple city of Varanasi on the banks of the holy River Ganges know it too. It is believed that the four rivers of creation flow down off the crown of Mount Kailas in Tibet, sacred mountain of the Buddhists, the Hindus, the Jainists. Climbing the mountain is forbidden; bathing in the rivers is holy. These rivers are the healing emissaries binding heaven to earth.

The Mississippi River isn't born of glacial fields on a sacred mountain, but of pure lake waters in Northern Minnesota. Two thousand miles later it empties, sullied and gigantic, into the Gulf of Mexico. Through the course of its life it carries the burden of a nation. All the rain and filth and dirt and debris from the tops of the Rockies to the tops of the Appalachians eventually end up here. It bears it all uncomplaining, on its tireless, substantial back. One day it casts it out to sea.

The Mississippi has been called upon throughout the ages. It can float a two-man raft as easily as a flatboat. It can spirit away a convict. It can cloak a runaway slave. It can generate a billion watts of electricity. When called upon to inspire, it inspires. When called upon to nourish, it nourishes.

In 1841 a whole people called upon the river for shelter. They came to one of its great, wide embraces, dredged the swamp on its shores, and carved out a city. They built a temple on a hill overlooking the river. Six years later, their city rivaled Chicago in population. The river sustained them, protected them. And when the people were forced to move west, and fast—the river *freed* them.

On February 24, 1846, Charles C. Rich became the first of many to *walk* across the great river. A miracle worker? Not quite. This river, pilgrim of the earth, helped these pilgrims of men and froze solid for days on end—a rare occurrence. Countless refugees escaped violent mobs by fleeing across the river into Iowa on its firm, unshakable back.

The city they built, and left, was Nauvoo; and Charles C. Rich, the man who walked across the river, testing the strength of the ice for the thousands that would follow, was our great-great-great-grandfather.

These days Nauvoo claims barely two thousand people, and survives largely on visits from history buffs who drop in to stroll through the restored streets. All that remained of the temple, which was destroyed in a tornado shortly after Charles C. Rich, Brigham Young, and everybody else left, was the limestone foundation. We sat on those stones and promised one day to return when the temple was rebuilt. Five years later, with the temple restored, we made good on our vow. But for now, the temple was a ghost, a distant memory.

Four days after Gary Kelley signed the Hero's Ball, we crossed the Mississippi into Illinois. A few miles south on State Route 91 we came to Nauvoo. At sunset we passed the temple's foundation, and then coasted down off the temple hill along a narrow road swarming with cottonwood blossoms. In the distance, a set of grain silos overlooked the river from the edge of a dock. We pulled to a stop where the water lapped against the dock and the fire shone on the water. We lay down our bikes at the brilliant, flaming edge of sunset.

During the last couple of days, we'd searched for a glimpse of the great river from the top of every corn-studded hill. We were so prematurely awed by the river's epic size that we expected to see it sparkling from a hundred miles away. I had suggested that upon arrival at its banks, we baptize ourselves as a communion with our country—and perhaps, like the impurities of America itself, allow the river to wash away our own lingering hang-ups.

Jared thought this was a very bad idea and warned that on the contrary, the river would likely infect us with a few hang-ups of its own—like toxic poisoning or malaria. Clint thought Jared was full of it, but he'd already had enough afflictions for one trip. So as I stood on the dock that evening, I realized this would be a solo plunge.

I was reminded of Sal Paradise's climactic journey in *On the Road*, which finds the travelers in the depths of Mexico. And Sal, unable to escape the insects and the heat, decides to embrace everything he has already tried to avoid, lies down on top of the car, and gets covered with bugs, blood, and sweat. "*The jungle takes you over and you become it.*"

The Mississippi embodies the bugs, the blood, and the sweat of our country. It is the pure and the impure, the mountain springs and the industrial waste. More than two hundred and fifty tributaries flow into it, carrying in their names the living prose of a nation: *Chippewa, Missouri, Kaskaskia, Ohio, Meramec, Arkansas* . . .

Jared and Clint were sitting on the dock a short distance away comparing mosquito bites. Alone, I watched the sunset across the waters. Our trip through America had been spectacular so far, and yet, like Sal, I longed for oneness with the "jungle."

My friends didn't notice as I stepped to the edge of the dock. Suddenly I had arrived at the centerpoint of my journey, the moment of communion. The waters below me may have sustained ranchers in Montana or farmers in South Dakota; they may have cooled condensers in the coal-fired generator plant in Genoa, Wisconsin, or hauled lumber from the mill in Clinton, Iowa. These waters may have filled swimming holes from Ohio to Colorado, or carried fifteen million tons of corn and wheat and coal from the Twin Cities to St. Louis. Ten thousand years ago these waters may have sustained Paleolithic hunters whose descendants would build sacred burial mounds near its shores.

As I stepped off the dock it felt as if I were suspended in air for a long time. Any lingering fears about the trip or the film vanished at once. Then the warm, oily depths enveloped me.

When I came back to the surface, Jared and Clint were staring down. Jared looked horrified.

"I can't believe you jumped in," he said.

"You guys gotta get in here," I said. "It feels great."

Clint looked longingly at the water. "You really think we'd get malaria?"

"Absolutely," said Jared.

"Hmm," said Clint.

34

"Look, you can see Iowa."

Night had fallen. Tiny lights blinked on across the river. All the shiny gold in the sky had faded to charcoal, and now the first stars appeared in the deepening firmament, and in the broad, dark waters beneath. Fireflies swarmed the forests near the dock, blinking on and off like Big Bang galaxies, little worlds beginning and ending—ten billion years collapsed into a half second.

The day gasped and life left it; it blessed the land with a final whisper, and then it was gone.

And the three of us sat together again on the edge of the dock—me a little wetter than the rest.

"I have an idea," said Clint.

"Yes, Clint."

"What do you guys think about this: What if we sorta postponed the bike trip for a while, built a raft, and floated to St. Louis?"

A beat-up copy of *Huck Finn*—which he'd begged for fifty cents from a used bookstore owner in Colorado—lay cracked open over his knee.

"Why not," said Jared.

"We could build it from scrap wood. There's gotta be a mill around here or something. We hook the bikes up, so we ride them, and it turns a wheel, you know, and it propels us forward."

None of us considered the Keokuk Dam nine miles down the road.

"You'll help me build it, right?"

"Of course, Clint."

One night in Ireland, three weeks after Cape Wrath, we met a chap on a hurlin' field where we planned to camp. Paddy was the caretaker of the field, and a proud caretaker at that. He came roaring up in his truck with his Irish temper flaring, having spotted us, uninvited, sprawled out on his beloved grass with our hairy chests and our ratted beards, with our gear and our flags, cooking up some Irish Sludge.

"We just wanted to see a hurlin' match," we said meekly before he could let fly the edict to be gone. "We've never seen one before."

And we watched as all the anger hissed out of him, as the laws of hometown pride and hospitality kicked in, and suddenly he's telling us all about what hurlin's like, and what the town's like, all about his family and red-haired Garrett who sat beside him in the truck, and then he said with great gusto, like a king throwing open the presidential suite: "Pitch yer tents anywhere you like!" He even tried our Sludge.

That night he and his pal Connie—thirty years, the best of friends!—returned to chaperone a teen dance in the recreation center at the far end of the field. And it was here, following a disappointing quest to a local pub to see "the greatest Elvis impersonator this side of Vegas!" that we struck up conversation.

"You want to learn some Gaelic, do you now?" said Connie, a teacher of the ancient speak at the local high school.

"This is the man to teach ya," boasted Paddy.

"Listen close now," said Connie, scribbling the magic words on the back of my notebook, "this is one of the oldest blessings in our language, and one of the most powerful . . ." He paused. "*Go neiri an bothar leat.*"

The words hung in the air like smoke and glowed on the page like fire. Magic words, old as the Irish hills. Words passed from generation to generation. I didn't know what they meant, but it seemed all the millions of times they'd been spoken coalesced around that one utterance— all the blessings and the hopes and the good feelings. And I felt the power of those words in my heart, though their meaning was still smoke.

"'*May the road rise with you,*' is what it means," said Paddy. And the smoke took form, and his eyes gleamed—because now the magic was passed on to me.

"The Irish are famous for their journeys," said Connie. "People give this blessing to pilgrims when they depart for their shrine. They've been doing it for hundreds of years."

I could have looked up Connie's blessing on the Internet anytime. But then it would have had no power. Passed from him to me—like it had been passed from friend to pilgrim for millennia—that is power.

I tried to pronounce it. "It takes a little time to get it right," said Connie. "The words have to be won, they have to be *believed* . . . then they'll sit on your tongue like a man on a tightwire."

"Is there a blessing you give?" Paddy asked.

"Well," I said, thinking back to an evening years ago on a great river, "there's something my friends and I say a lot when we go on pilgrimages. It doesn't quite have the romance of *May the road rise with you,* and it's more of a mantra, but it works for us."

"What is it?" asked Connie.

"*Whatever happens is best,*" I said.

And now my words hung on the air—spoken fewer times than theirs, but spoken still, and meant sincerely every time. And they were believed, as we'd come to believe them, on journeys far and wide, just as *Go neiri an bother leat* was believed, and believed *in*, over countless centuries, and countless journeys.

Connie and Paddy scratched their stubbled chins and examined the words as they hung, like smoke, between us. "It sounds like the same thing," said Paddy.

"It is the same," said Connie.

Whatever happens is best. For us, the most magical of all pilgrim mantras, perhaps even more magical than *We rolled in real late last night.*

But this mantra is no excuse for idleness. *Whatever happens is best* only if you act—only if you seek. One moment of looking back and the mantra is broken. Like those street rappers who rap from the hip. A word is spoken; a rhyme must be found. A pilgrimage or a rhyme: each is an act of faith and skill.

"Now let me get your picture for me website," said Paddy after the lessons were through and the words had faded. Connie and I crammed in close to each other. "Ahh, that's nice. We don't get many Americans biking through town, you know."

Now the blackness over the river was complete. Blackness clear and beautiful, studded with stars, serenaded with crickets, hushed by a breeze. Barges crawled up and down the river, the water sang against the side of the dock; more than five thousand universes had begun and ended during the past fifteen minutes.

We rode back through town and camped beneath a massive oak tree on a hill overlooking a tiny pond, part of the farm owned by Mr. Jerry McLeod. One of his daughters, Tuesday, had invited us over when we first rolled into town. Mr. McLeod hadn't been too thrilled at her offer of hospitality—his daughter was always inviting over eligible single guys for substantial stays. But McLeod turned out to be one of our truest friends of the trip, full of enough wisdom and stories to fill a whole summer, let alone a few days.

35

The next day I got a job moving hotel furniture around. Despite the economic miracles of Sludge, peanut butter sandwiches, and the True Fan Discount, our money had evaporated. While Jared and Clint buzzed around town, I spent the day with a guy named Bob. The first day we mostly small-talked. The next day, during a drive along the river road to Hamilton, Bob opened up. "I've lived a hard life," he confided. "I've had many life experiences. I've had more life experiences than three people my same age." I asked him to elaborate.

Bob had been married three times. His second wife had turned their one daughter against him completely. She wouldn't even talk to him anymore. "Then I got involved with a church in Massachusetts," he continued. "The reverend had a lot of energy, a lot of charisma. People were really drawn to him. He collected over forty thousand dollars from all of us for a new church, and then one night he ran off with the secretary. That was the last we saw of him." Bob had lost a few hundred dollars; others had lost thousands. "But it was the loss of trust that hurt," he added.

"I've seen suffering too. I served in Korea and Vietnam; I spent over twenty years running around the world watching people die. I don't know why I didn't go right along with them. I always wonder that." Somehow, he'd ended up in Nauvoo.

"There's something out there for me," he said soberly, staring down the road. "I just haven't found it yet."

"What do you think that something is?" I asked.

"I don't know. I'm having a bit of a tug-of-war with God right now," he said, motioning to the Camel Lights on the dash. "There's a few things He wants me to give up, but I'm not quite ready yet."

One evening a few days later, Bob invited the three of us over for some lemonade. He introduced his wife and daughter, hugging them fiercely. *Let it work this time, please God.* After all the betrayal, it seemed he clung to their trust as if it were the only thing that kept him believing.

Mr. McLeod, our Nauvoo host, was another man who'd seen his share of suffering. Every morning when we got up we'd watch him come to the edge of his pond and throw bread crumbs to his fish. McLeod wasn't one to talk much, but after a few days on his lawn, he warmed up to us. I walked down with my camera while he was feeding the fish one morning and asked him about his life. "Why did you join the Marines?" I asked.

"Because my brother said I couldn't take it." He stared at me with this look that said: *But I did take it; oh, I suffered, but dammit all, did I take it.*

"How many years?"

"Thirty-one. Korea when I was eighteen, Vietnam when I was thirty-four. And all spots in between." Like Bob, McLeod's life had been far from a bed of roses. One of his daughters was a real spitfire. "Yancy's favorite thing to do is climb to the top of that tree there," he nodded at the huge, dead oak rising from the banks of the pond. "She climbs to the top and dives from the highest branch."

"Is the pond deep enough?"

"Oh, it's deep enough . . . if you hit the water in the right spot." The tree was topping sixty feet. McLeod probably used to worry, but not anymore. He'd gotten used to it.

"One night we got home from a movie and found every piece of glass in the house broken. It was Yancy's boyfriend. He got a little jealous. It was one of his hobbies."

McLeod threw a few more crumbs to the fish. I let the camera roll. "The mind's a strange thing," he said. "I guess it's because you try to forget the hard times and the bad things, and all you remember is the good times that you've had. In Vietnam, there were hard times, but there were a lot of things to laugh at too. Like when the cobras would stand up in the middle of the path and everybody would run . . . One kid jumped up on a radio van and didn't come down for eight months."

I wondered if Mr. McLeod still believed there was *something out there for him.* I didn't think so. I think his search had led him within, transporting him every morning to the edge of his pond where life became clear after a few crumbs of bread.

"I went to church one Sunday and the chaplain about fainted, because he thought he had just put me in a body bag and sent me home. It was someone that looked like me, I guess . . . And that's hard to believe, that anybody in this world would look like me." McLeod looks like no one else on earth. (If you don't believe me, watch my movie.)

We took a few turns flying off the rope swing (connected to Yancy's daredevil tree) into the pond. Mr. McLeod became frustrated with our neophyte efforts and instructed us on the proper way of swinging out: "You gotta swing so your legs go up and you slip right down into the water." Nobody could get it right.

Five years later when we returned to Nauvoo to see the temple dedicated, we visited Mr. McLeod's pond, and the tree was gone.

"What happened?" we asked.

"Well, we had a big fellow staying with us last summer [undoubtedly somebody Tuesday had invited over], real big, three hundred and fifty pounds, I reckon . . . He took a swing out into the pond and pulled the whole tree down with him."

One week after arriving in Nauvoo, the road began to call to us again. I looked in the mirror that morning and searched for the thousand-mile stare. I saw the stare all right, but I also saw a sense of calm I had not seen all trip.

We left Nauvoo on the morning of August 1, striking off across the flat, tranquil plains of Central Illinois.

"I think maybe we'll float the Mississippi next summer," said Clint. *Huck Finn* poked up just above the lip of his handlebar-supported front pouch. He finished it three days ago, and was reading it again.

"I'm on board," I said.

"Count me in," said Jared.

The wide, impossibly huge sphere of the earth and sky opened around us. We felt its gigantic breadth, we saw the clock face unlatch, and witnessed the mechanics of creation, first unveiled in Eastern Colorado, surrounding us again: corn, soy, sprinklers, and these odd, little oval-shaped clouds, floating just above the road.

"Somebody somewhere right now is looking up there and saying: Look—UFOs!" laughed Jared as we wove in and out of the dashes and saw no cars for a million miles straight out in either direction.

We lost ourselves deep in the magic fields of Illinois.

We had no idea that very soon, we would be called upon to work a miracle.

36

Not many books have been written about the town of Dawson, Illinois. Not many films have been shot there. Not one person in a thousand could find it on a map. It is as anonymous as little towns come, tucked away in the corn, twenty miles east of Springfield in the heart of Lincoln's land. It has a park; it has nice grass. It has tidy houses lining tidy streets, surrounded by fields of epic size. These endless fields call to boys and girls when they start to grow—like the ocean calls to children on the coasts and the mountains call to children in the high country. The fields, the oceans, the mountains—they never stop calling, until the children shut out the Voice and can't hear it anymore, like the children and the bell in *The Polar Express*—or, they accept the call and strike off one day across those fields to see just how big they are.

Around nine o'clock on August 3, we rolled into the Christmas Eve quiet of Dawson. Down where the town ended and the cornfields began, we found a park—and a shrine. Clint hadn't shown us his Perfect Hoop clipping for a while, probably because he was finding it everyday in one-hundred-year-old hoops hanging by rusty hooks from barn doors; in an abandoned schoolyard court in Grand Island, Nebraska, with weeds running up the limitless cracks in the ancient cement. But this court, this shrine, was special; you could feel it. The moment you stepped across the threshold, the world went quiet and clear, time itself crystallizing like fresh-fallen snow on gaunt branches at first light.

I tossed the ball out of the Ark. Clint took the pass and started shooting around. From everywhere he popped, the ball knew its destination. This pilgrim had made up its mind. It wasn't going anywhere but in.

Clint's shooting was so remarkable that a couple kids came over to watch. Their names were Josh and Josh. Josh the First was fifteen years old, dark-haired, dark-eyed. He had a solemn face and didn't smile, didn't laugh, and didn't think Clint was all that impressive. He reminded me of the distant side of Wael. Josh the Second was fourteen years old, blond, inquisitive—he still had a touch of childhood innocence that was entirely lost on his darker, older friend.

"If you're so good," said Josh the First, "hit one from here." A modest challenge, just a twenty-five-footer. Clint dribbled the ball to where he stood and drained it.

"Not bad," said the First Josh.

"Lucky," said the Second Josh. "Try this one." He stepped back another couple feet. Clint sunk that shot too.

"Wow, do you play, like, college or something?" I thought back to Coach Nielson's list on the wall.

"No," said Clint, "I just love the game."

Josh the Second walked over to the side of the court. "How about from here." Easy. Jared and I rebounded. He was in the zone tonight; he was lost to the court. The Two Joshes fed him a few more challenges. Clint answered every one.

"You sure you didn't play college?"

"I almost didn't play high school."

Our senior year he moved to Kingman, Arizona, to live with his dad. Trying out for a new team in a new town mid-season is just not done, but the coach had heard of Clint, gave him a shot, and he made it.

On their first road trip, Clint and the rest of the team were riding the bus to the game when one of the guys noticed Clint didn't have the team shoe, retail ninety bucks. "There's no way I can afford it," he told the coach. His dad was renting a room in a dumpy motel and the best he could do was a pair of nine-dollar Wal-Mart specials.

Four hours later at Clint's first game of varsity ball, he found a new pair of shoes sitting on the bench. "Whose are these?" he asked.

"They're yours," said the coach. "The guys and I pooled some money. If you're gonna play on this team, you gotta wear the right shoes."

Clint drilled Josh the Second's latest challenge, a half-court heave. The Two Joshes shook their heads in amazement. Even Josh the First was starting to crack. But I think Clint could tell that the boys needed something extra tonight, a pinch of the miraculous. So, once he was done with their little games, he took the ball, marched past the three-point stripe, past the half-court line, to the place where the concrete met the corn, marched off into the corn until you couldn't even see him anymore, turned around, and said, "What do you give me if I hit a shot from here?"

Josh the First laughed; clearly, he thought Clint was out of his mind. Even Jared and I thought he was out of his mind. The zone is one thing, but this . . . "If I hit this shot," said Clint, "you guys make us breakfast tomorrow."

"Good freaking luck," said Josh the First.

"All right, breakfast," said Josh the Second. They didn't even ask what would happen if he *didn't* make the shot—the humiliation would be prize enough.

Now there were three main challenges to the shot. First of all, it was very, very dark—so dark Clint could barely see the rim from the foul line, let alone the cornfield. Second, it was very, very far. Clint would be hard-pressed to heave the ball that far, let alone shoot it. And finally, the corn was so tall, the only way he could see the hoop would be to jump above it. So, Clint wouldn't even be able to see his target until he was well on his way to releasing the shot.

Clint spun the ball in his hands a few times until he got the grip he wanted. Everyone fell quiet, including the Two Joshes. And then he rose like a ghost from the corn. He released the ball off the tips of his fingers, at the top of his jump. And that ol' ball sailed through the heartland sky, past all the constellations and galaxies, traveling the entire span of the Milky Way. And the four of us watched it fly in reverent amazement. Because despite the dark, despite the corn, despite the fact that it was really, really far, that ball had a shot at the impossible.

The ball hit the top of its arc and began to fall. And it fell and it fell, back-spinning, dropping, falling, and—

"Pancakes," said Clint, as he emerged from the corn, "with raspberry syrup and orange juice."

Well, word got around pretty quick that *the Greatest Ball Player* in the history of the Dawson town courts had just hit *the Greatest Shot* in the history of the Dawson town courts. Clint was besieged by teenaged disciples, and, true to his wish at Big Bear Lake, was teaching his awestruck followers the finer points of rolling a basketball up and down their arms. As he passed around the ball he asked them, "So, what do you guys do in Dawson?"

"Nothing," said the First Josh.

"There's nothing to do here," said the Second Josh.

"Nothing to do here!" said Clint. "You can look for shooting stars!"

"I've never seen a shooting star," said the First Josh.

"Me neither," said the Second. The rest of the kids concurred; nobody had seen a shooting star.

We couldn't believe it. "People in the city would kill for a sky like this!" Growing up, we'd spent every summer night lying on the trampoline in the backyard, scouring the heavens. Our dad knew every constellation, thanks to a thousand nights under the stars in the Uinta Mountains or the Wasatch. Never seen a shooting star? Tragic.

Clint immediately ordered everyone to lie down on the grass and every kid obeyed. You do not defy the wishes of the Great One, after all.

The night sky was huge and perfect: no moon, no clouds, and the stars were bright. To the west, the distant glow of Springfield washed out the sky just a bit.

"Nothing's happening," said Josh the First.

"You gotta give it time," said Clint.

One of the kids got up to go. Clint ordered him to lie back down.

We watched in silence. And sure enough, not two minutes later, a nice gash opened up just above the Summer Triangle. All the kids *oohed*. "Now there's something to do in Dawson," Clint said.

"We can come out here all the time!" exploded the Second Josh. "We can bring girls out here!" Everyone was excited about the prospects, and went into details about which girls they wanted to bring and when. Just that fast, everything had changed.

We watched for shooting stars for a long time. A while later, Clint gave a final few basketball pointers, and all the kids drifted off to their homes. Alone, the three of us gathered around the picnic table and fired up the campstove for a few rounds of hot chocolate. "I just gotta tell you, Clint, that was some shot," Jared said.

"Do you think they're really gonna bring us breakfast?" I said. Jared shook his head. Clint looked at him like he'd been betrayed. "Well, of course they're going to bring us breakfast!"

"No way," said Jared.

"But I hit the shot." It was that simple for Clint. He'd hit the shot, he'd won the bet, and now pancakes and orange juice were on the way.

And sure enough, the next morning at the crack of dawn, Josh the Second came rolling up on his beat-up dirt bike with a stack of plates under his arm. He threw the plates, a stack of pancakes, some syrup, and a fistful of genuine silverware across the table. "Don't steal the silverware," he said. "My mom'd be pissed."

"Where's Josh the First?"

"Probably sleeping in. He was supposed to bring the OJ."

Josh the Second had some chores to do, and was gone before he'd even had time to sign the Hero's Ball.

Clint drowned his flapjacks in syrup. "Mmmm, I do love pancakes. Yessiree."

I forked a couple, followed hesitantly by Jared. "Dig in, Jare; I forgive your lack of faith."

"Well, this is one for the books," he muttered.

As we ate the pancakes I thought back to high school, back to the shot that didn't go in for our varsity team in the state finals, the shot Clint should have made.

I guess, like I said before, he was just saving it up for a later day.

37

In 1831, New Salem was as anonymous a town as Dawson. Founded two years before, it boasted a population of five hundred, claimed a ramshackle collection of houses, a few businesses, and infamously muddy streets. But it was here that a young deckhand as anonymous as the town landed and decided to stay. It was here, in this tiny hamlet, that he transformed himself into perhaps our country's greatest hero.

We rolled into New Salem, Illinois, around eight o'clock on a warm, electric night. Thunderstorms were on the way, a good distance off at the moment, but they were coming. We didn't even know what New Salem *was* back then. But we were delighted, after finding a nice campground, to stumble across an amphitheater and watch the homegrown musical, *Abraham!*

The musical opens with Abraham Lincoln's arrival in New Salem on a barge floating down the Sangamon River. At the time he was nothing more than "an aimless piece of driftwood" (as he called himself) who found his way to this little town and decided to stay. He picked up a job at a local store, proved his mettle in a much-celebrated wrestling match, devoured a library of books, began his study of law, led the local militia, and within six years had transformed himself into a promising statesman. It was in New Salem that Abraham Lincoln came to believe in himself.

At the end of the show, with the music swelling, Lincoln bids his friends farewell and walks right out of town, out of the amphitheater, bound for Springfield twenty miles to the south, and eventually, the White House. But coming to New Salem was the thing that changed him.

The morning after the Breakfast Shot, I was lying in the grass after eating those tasty pancakes, and the strangest feeling came over me. I wrote in my journal:

> *It was as if for a moment I was allowed to step back from the whole event and see these glorious three and a half months in retrospect. And what I gathered from this stepping back was the impression that I simply don't, and at this moment,* can't *grasp the importance of this trip.*

You can feel the road working on you, but you'll never have any idea just how much it will impact you until time begins to pass.

Lincoln left New Salem in 1837 and came to the aid of our country in its darkest hour. He rode away on a borrowed horse with everything he owned contained in two saddlebags. Everyone has a pilgrimage to make.

We never found out what became of the Two Joshes, but I'm betting that for the Second, there's a pilgrimage in store. You could sense the call of those endless fields echoing inside him; and you could sense something in him change when the Breakfast Shot sailed home.

Josh the Second would have been the forty-first True Fan to sign our Hero's Ball; for every Hero that signed, there were two more that rode away. Everywhere we turned somebody was showing us their true greatness—like one afternoon in the Eagle Grocery Store in Decatur, Illinois, the day after the Breakfast Shot.

We were sitting inside on a bench, taking a break from the oppressive heat, when suddenly a funny old woman approached us, hunkered down in our faces, and with the most intense look in her eyes said, "Do you need anything?"

None of us knew what to say. "Do you need anything?" she asked again. *Something—anything.* "How about your clothes? They're dirty . . . you need them washed, right? You must be hungry, right? You need a place to stay tonight, right?"

We shrugged and said, "Right."

"Well then, you've got to come over to my house," she said, standing up and whipping out a notepad. She wrote the address on a page and tore it out. "We'll have a great big dinner, we can get all your laundry done, and then . . . and then"—and you could tell that here was the good stuff—"then we'll take you down to Krekel's for some of the best custard in the country."

Louise Parsons and her husband Jess were retired folks living a quiet life in a quiet neighborhood. Louise immediately confiscated our sweaty gear and, without so much as a disparaging glance, tossed it all into the washer.

"When our kids were in Europe people took such great care of them, we've always wanted to repay the favor," said Louise. Once again we witnessed the transitive nature of Heroism. Like the teenagers in Utah who'd brought us POWERades.

"What's life like in Decatur?" We asked as we sat around the table, enjoying the sort of meat-and-potatoes feast available only in the heartland. We'd noticed the tossed classifieds and the run-down factories. Louise and Jess just smiled.

"We've got some unemployment problems; there are some violent parts of town. These poor folks, they just get so frustrated—and you can't blame them. There isn't much work here; times aren't what they used to be in Decatur. But we've got a great parks system, we've got a rich history, and Krekel's . . . You're going to love Krekel's."

Down at Krekel's the whole town was out, and it seemed Louise knew everyone. She started chatting with a cop standing next to us. You'd think they were lifelong friends. "Never met him before in her life," said Jess with an admiring smile. "That's just the way she is."

As Louise was talking with the cop, Jess told us a story. "Louise and one of our sons were in New York one time and this homeless man approached them, asking for money. Our son was a little put off and tried to move on, but Louise noticed a cut on the guy's hand, grabbed it, and said, 'My goodness! You've got to do something about this!' Louise is a nurse, so she's always got a few things with her. She stopped right there, cleaned the wound, and wrapped it up with gauze."

Two years later when I finally premiered my film *True Fans* in a woodland amphitheater in the mountains above Salt Lake City, who should show up but Louise and Jess Parsons, acting like Utah was just around the block. "We just drove out to hear the concert tonight and see the movie," said Louise matter-of-factly.

We all slept in an upstairs loft, so quiet—and even a little sad, it seemed—what with the kids all gone. We could sense them there, though; the memories . . . the ghosts.

The next day the Parsonses signed our Hero's Ball and we left the land of Lincoln behind.

38

"If the Perfect Hoop exists," Jared said, as we sailed through the wooded hills of Indiana, "this is where we'll find it."

Somewhere between Paris and Indianapolis, between Fort Wayne and Evansville, somewhere deep in the mythical geography of basketball's grassroots homeland, the Perfect Hoop stands stoically beside a tree of epic size and grandeur.

"I disagree," said Clint. "It's gotta be down by the ocean."

"But this is Indiana, man—this is like the spiritual center of basketball!"

Clint leaned back on his saddle, shaking his head, arms stretched out into the air as the little hills roller-coastered us through the green, sun-lit wood. "True," said Clint, "but the Perfect Hoop is by the ocean. You saw the seagull."

A great barn rose from the trees; we saw it at the last minute and felt that familiar tug. We turned off down a gravel path, rounded a corner near a farmhouse, and when the barn came into view—so did the shrine.

"I knew it," I said.

The hoop had been nailed to the peeling face of the gigantic barn decades ago. A tattered net still hung from the eyelets. The grass was cut short beneath it, pounded hard and flat by years of playing.

We shot around for a few minutes before the curious owner, an architect in his fifties, ambled over to see what was going on. When you're on a pilgrimage and have nothing, little things like property ownership just don't make much difference.

"You've got a great hoop here," said Clint.

"Kids haven't shot around on that thing for years," he said, a little embarrassed about the weeds scaling the barn. "It's nice to see it getting some use again."

"Yeah, I'm sure there were some battles here . . ."

He nodded quietly and offered us some lemonade.

Indiana is to basketball what Wisconsin is to cheese. Legendary for high school standouts and college powerhouses, it is filled with more hoops per capita than any other state. Whether this is truth, or another manifestation of the "Be Scared" phenomenon, we may never know. Whatever it is, the spirit of the game seems to preside over everything here; you almost expect to wake up in the middle of the night and see teams of long-dead greats launching full-court games up and down the breadth of the sky.

39

"If the Perfect Hoop does in fact exist in Indiana," said Clint as we crossed the Ohio line, "it will have to be the subject of a future excursion."

On August 10, the day after leaving Indiana, we rolled into famous Ten Fountain Square in Cincinnati in the early afternoon. Before we even had time to dismount we were accosted by the caretaker. Like Kenny Shaw and Richard Bennett, this anonymous hero also took immense pride in his work.

"Welcome to Cincinnati!" he exclaimed. "It's a great city—a great city! We got problems like anybody else, but there are a lot of things we do really well." He had been cleaning up the square with all his heart for more than forty years.

The caretaker reminded me of a quote I'd once read from the Reverend Martin Luther King Jr.:

> If a man is called to be a streetsweeper, he should sweep streets even as Michelangelo painted, or Beethoven composed music, or Shakespeare wrote poetry. He should sweep streets so well that all the hosts of heaven and earth will pause to say, here lived a great streetsweeper who did his job well.

This, we were coming to believe, was at the heart of Heroism—embracing whatever you have chosen to make of your life and doing it well. *Heroically.* The happiest people we met on our journey were not the rich people, the poor people, the people who lived in the mountains, or those who lived near the sea. The happiest people were those who did whatever they did with competence and joy—those who practiced their own unique Heroic Expression. People like the creators of the musical *Abraham!*, two fellows who were so gracious when we met them after the show. People like the farmers we'd been waving to since Colorado. People like the plaza caretaker we met that day in Cincinnati.

"I've got six children and ten grandbabies," he said, beaming, "and I love 'em all." Then he ran around and gathered up his co-workers, his boss, and everybody else he knew to meet these three guys going cross-country on their bikes.

Ten minutes later the nice folks in the Rock Bottom Brewery bought us lunch. We sat out in the sunshine and listened to a show going on in the square. America was abounding with Heroism—it was practically busting at the seams! A few folks in the West had warned us that, "Once you cross the Mississippi River, people change." And not for the better, they meant. But we were finding exactly the opposite to be true. People everywhere wanted to be Heroes. And if given the chance, they'd take it.

While riding along the Ohio River the next day, two Kentucky melon farmers nodded us over to their roadside stand. The mist was rising off the road—then falling again—like a balloon with fading helium, and the air was thick and warm.

"These are the finest melons on earth," they said. They gave us one, then another, then the older guy said, "Hell, load up their little trailer with melons, they won't get sick of 'em." To these melon farmers this was their Heroic Expression, equal to any other.

I always wondered growing up in Utah why they called them "honeydews." That night in Augusta, slicing melons on the shores of the Ohio River, I found out.

A couple days later we rolled into West Virginia through the industrial town of Huntington. Outside a major coal mine, an old man came up to us. He asked us what we were doing and we told him.

"That's right—see the country, see how good we got it," he said.

Mining is not an easy profession, and Dick Simmons had been doing it his whole life. His fingernails were so destroyed by hard labor they looked like chunks of wood grafted on to the edge of his fingers. But nothing could have dimmed the pride he took in his work. He did what he did well—Heroically. To him, mining was an act of Heroic Expression, and his act was equal to any other. No matter how grand or humble, you do all you can with what you have—and that is enough.

"I don't have a lot of money," he said, "but I've got a little, and I can give some away." He gave me five bucks—a dirty, coal-streaked five-dollar bill.

Dick Simmons signed the Ball.

Two nights later we were in Charleston, West Virginia's elegant capital. Jared was especially paranoid tonight, begging to get out of town and find a nice patch of church lawn beyond the perils of thieves, gangs, and murderers. We were in Wendy's, supplementing our fourth round of peanut butter sandwiches with trip favorite Frosties. Clint and I tried to reassure him. "Jared, really, we'll be fine."

"How do you know? Really, how do you know?" His fear was so tangible it began to infect me, and I wondered if maybe there *was* something to fear after all. You don't naturally fear unless given a reason. I locked myself in the Wendy's bathroom and decided I wasn't leaving until I got this figured out.

I sat in that bathroom for a good twenty minutes, and then it came to me: It didn't matter. It didn't matter what I chose. Faith is faith. *Whatever happens is best*. You choose your *spiritual path* and the physical one will take care of itself. Just make a decision and stick with it. Go to the church and don't look back, or stick around downtown and don't look back. Let the road rise with you.

"All right, Jare, let's go find the church."

The nearest church was four miles away; at least, that's the one Jared wanted to camp at because it was "a safe distance from downtown." We needed a few supplies first, so we popped into a grocery store to load up. And here we met John Buckant.

"Welcome to West Virginia—glad to have ya!" he said. John wore a Harley-Davidson T-shirt and ten grand in gold chains around his neck. He drove a Mercedes convertible. He came over and asked us what we were doing. We told him about the trip, about the last few days battling rain as we'd jumped back and forth across the Ohio.

"Well, listen. I've got a real nice place down by the river, great big house, and we just installed a new Jacuzzi last night. You guys can break it in a little better tonight!"

Half an hour later, in the golden hour just after sunset when the world is most quiet, we were riding along the river. There were couples kissing on the grass, walking along the water, enjoying the evening.

"Why does it always work out like that?" asked Jared, still stunned. "We either got some big-time deity working overtime for us, or we're just luckier 'n hell." Jared prattled on about how this could be possible for the next twenty minutes. Faith is just not very pragmatic when you get right down to it. He was still shaking his head when we rolled up to John Buckant's mansion just after dark.

"This is the best hot tub money can buy. You got two jets on your shoulders and two on the back of your neck. This'll fix you up all right for tonight!"

We didn't shower; we just hopped in. I'm sure John was cleaning mosquito repellent from York, Nebraska, and grime from that flat tire in Maysville, Kentucky, out of the filter for weeks to come, but man, did it feel good. We watched TV on the big screen all night, and slept on leather couches downstairs. The next day Clint took John's Harley for a spin around the corner and everybody got to meet John's miniature poodle, Shatzy.

"Do your Harley buddies know you have a poodle?" we asked.

"They know I have a dog," he said, "but they don't know what kind." We walked down to his private dock and cruised up the river.

Life was good for John. Thirteen years ago he'd contracted bone cancer in his hand, lost a finger, and nearly lost his life. "Then I found out my wife was seeing my best friend. That turned my life upside down pretty good."

After beating cancer and getting a divorce, he took custody of his three children. "I was washing diapers, running kids around to day care, working twelve-hour shifts. There weren't enough hours in the day."

But then things began to look up. He credited the sudden turn-around to a renewed appreciation for life, infused in him after he'd chosen to let his faith sustain him once the emotional and physical cancers had passed.

"I always believed in a Higher Power," he said as we passed the stunning, gold-domed West Virginia capitol. "I didn't *need* a Higher Power, but I believed in one. After the cancer, I *needed* a Higher Power.

"And heck," he said, holding up his right hand as he steered the boat with his left, "nine's almost as good as ten."

John gave us a few bucks for the road and signed the Ball. We got off in the early afternoon and stopped at another Wendy's for lunch. The manager saw us bike in and comped the meal. Jared had given up trying to explain our luck—he just sat there shaking his head as he devoured his chicken sandwich.

It was Friday night. The road to Glen Ferris was wild, narrow, and full of drunk drivers.

After a good, hard grind the hills opened up, the sky opened up, the road widened, and we found ourselves on a wide jog of the Kanawha River, almost more like a bay. The moon was on the water; the night was hazy and mysterious.

We flung ourselves at the mercy of two waitresses at the Glen Ferris Inn with soothing, sexy southern drawls. They couldn't believe we'd biked so far, and they brought us a feast of leftovers—another free meal. We hadn't paid for a bite to eat (save a Frosty) in more than three days.

We camped that night on the shores of the river, right next to the road.

40

The next morning as we were packing up, a door opened across the street. A woman called out to us. "What are you boys doing down there?"

"We just camped out," we said.

"Well, why don't you come over for breakfast in a half hour or whenever you're ready." The old woman lived with her husband and their angry little dog. Mr. Robinson was a retired dean of math at a nearby college. He asked us all sorts of questions about our "pilgrimage."

"I went on a pilgrimage once," he said slowly. Mr. Robinson had Parkinson's, and it rendered him almost immobile.

"I was in the military during World War Two, and I was stationed in China." *Sometimes you choose the Key Journey, and sometimes the Key Journey chooses you*, I thought. "Well, I was born in the South, you know, Alabama. And we were brought up to hate black people. Hell, we were brought up to hate anybody that wasn't white—Mexicans, Asians, ethnic people, anybody different than us." He paused to take a couple slow, deep breaths. His wife watched, unable to conceal the worry that had attended her for some time.

"In those days I used to have an afternoon where I ran errands out through the countryside. Sometimes I liked to take a scenic route back. One time I came across this group of Chinese schoolchildren on their way home, and I stopped the car and watched them. And as I watched, these kids tussled and played and teased each other just like any white kid in America. 'My God!' I thought. 'They're just like us!'"

When Mr. Robinson returned home from the war, he tried to convince his fourteen brothers and sisters of what he'd found. "About half of them believed me; the other half wanted to hang me." That's why he left his hometown, and that's why to this day, Mr. Robinson is never shy when it comes to voicing his opinions about racial equity—or anything else, for that matter.

"Do you believe in God?" he asked us. We said that we did.

"Well, I don't."

"What happens when you die?"

He made an umpire's safe sign with his hands. "That's it—game over."

"Did you always believe this way?"

"Oh no," he said. "I was raised to fear God, to fear God with all my heart. One day when I was about twelve, I was out in the field working, and I hit myself with a shovel. I said, 'Goddammit!' before I could stop myself. Then I cowered on the ground, fully expecting God to strike me down. But God never did. I stood up and thought: Huh—there must not be a God."

41

Ten years before our trip across America, I was in Scotland with my mom. It was the Fourth of July. My mom was giving a paper at a conference in Dublin, but we had a few days to burn first. Since those Iowa days, we'd become great friends. Nothing enhances a friendship like a pilgrimage.

We were walking down the streets of Edinburgh in the heart of the city when we saw an old postcard seller standing on the corner. He wore a tattered gray coat repaired in many places, an old pair of glasses, and, oddly enough, a Stetson. But what really drew our attention was a handwritten cardboard sign affixed to the side of his stand. It read: CHARLIE WELCOMES ALL AMERICANS ON THE 4TH OF JULY!

As soon as Charlie saw us walking over, you'd think he was greeting long-lost friends. "Americans! Happy Fourth of July!"

"We saw your sign."

"I put it up every year."

"Did you used to live in America?"

"Well, I'll tell you the story," he said, and he took a deep breath and squared his shoulders—as if this were a story deserving the very best recitation.

"You see, I fought in World War Two and I was injured in battle. They brought me to America to get better. I wore my kilt and the official uniform of the Scottish contingent to the Armed Forces, and all the Americans thought I was a hero. I rode in a parade! One man came up to me and said, 'You need to have something from Texas to take back to Scotland with you!' And he took the hat off his head and gave it to me. And since that day I have worn my hat and put up my sign every July Fourth."

"Morning, Charlie," said a man as he passed.

"Morning, James." The postcard seller seemed to know everyone.

We looked through his postcards and selected a few—a few more than we needed; we wanted to help him out. He told us he had seven children and twice as many grandchildren, many of whom he was still helping to support. But when we went to pay, the postcard seller would hear none of it. "Oh no, not today. You take them with you—they are yours. My gift to you on the Fourth of July."

We tried to convince him to let us pay, but he was resolute. As we walked away that morning, I vowed that one day I would return to Edinburgh on the Fourth of July to see if there was anything I could do in return for the postcard seller.

Thirteen years later to the day, I met my brothers in Edinburgh. They'd started biking in London and had been on the road for two weeks. Micah was still using the pen my dad had given him in the airport.

We searched all afternoon for the postcard seller, but he was gone. Most people remembered him, however: "Aye, I remember. Haven't seen 'im for years. He used to stand on that corner over there, selling postcards and smiling at everyone."

A wise bike shop owner back in Huntington had told us that we'd never have any idea the sort of effect we were having on the people around us. "People see what you're doing and they say to themselves: Now what do *I* really want to do with my life? It gets 'em thinkin'. That's how it begins."

A few postcards on a sunny day bought me Cape Wrath and that night on the hurlin' field, learning Gaelic. Not to mention a new closeness with my brothers. Ten minutes of interaction with a total stranger more than a decade before rippled back to give me the exuberant, healing journey I needed, exactly when I needed it. Things like this happen, and you begin to wonder if every single blade of grass is somehow in on the gig.

42

We-mean-business clouds were ganging up overhead, and from far away over the green hills and mountains, trembled deep-throated rumblings that sounded like the rind of the earth itself getting peeled.

"Jared, honestly, it's only seventeen cents."

"I think they'll understand," said Clint, glancing off in the direction of the rumblings.

"But it's a matter of principle."

The thunder came up again, a little closer.

"Well, hurry then."

It doesn't cost a lot to refill your campstove, but Jared had forgotten to pay. We were making for the Summit Lake campground about five miles away, and if we hurried, we could beat the rain. *If* we hurried.

Clint tensed up as the thunder sounded, closer still. "Hurry, Jare, hurry little guy." Clint was not liking the rain much these days; we'd been trapped in this rainy prison for nearly two weeks, and everything was soaked. Save for that one auspicious night turning to mush in John Buckant's hot tub, there had been no reprieve.

Clint gripped his handlebars, staring down the road where Jared had disappeared. It was a mile back to town, but he'd dumped his gear. It shouldn't take him long, right?

"Dan, I really don't want to get wet anymore."

"We're not gonna get wet, Clint, take it easy."

Just to be cautious, Clint hopped off his bike and meticulously covered his panniers with those NASA-designed, yellow rain-covers that came with the packs. The guy in the bike shop in LA had talked them up pretty good: "Oh yeah, you could ride through a *monsoon* with these things!" They were, of course, utterly useless. Even so, Clint was determined to squeeze every cent out of his purchase and would abruptly pull over at the slightest rainy provocation, hop off his bike, and pull the rain-covers over his bags. The first time this happened, Jared nearly ran him over; then I nearly ran them *both* over; then, as the rain bore down on all of us, Jared and I got a little upset because, "Dammit, Clint, if it weren't for those stupid rain-covers, we could be under that tree over there by now!"

Clint ignored us, delicately tucking tab A under fold B. Jared and I quickly learned neither to argue nor complain—the sooner Clint completed the task, the sooner we could go. Clint would sit there, focused and concentrating, until every inch of ripstop Cordura was covered.

Clint was about halfway home with his task when Jared reappeared. He skidded to a stop and threw on his panniers. "This storm's a real doozy," he said. "Everybody in the gas station was talking about it."

For the first time, Clint didn't fully secure his rain-covers. In a flash we were flying off into the mountains.

Three miles up the road the thunder was close enough to shake the leaves from the trees. A terse wind came up and a few heavy drops scattered across the road like tiddlywinks. We found the Summit Lake turnoff and bolted up the road. Each time the thunder sounded now, it was closer. The wind was hitting us from all sides; the trees shuddered. The rain would be upon us in a heartbeat. There was only one thing we could do: unleash the strongest legs in America.

"Jare!" I yelled. "Run up the road and get the tent set up before it hits—I don't think we're gonna make it."

Jared nodded and was off. Clint and I watched him go in wonder, as we always did. Jared's got the skinniest legs I've ever seen, but pound-for-pound, the strongest. Clint, carrying the same weight with his pile-driver thighs, could not compete.

Halfway up to the lake an old Cadillac in mint condition came flying down the road and passed us in a *hush* of spray. It looked like a silvery apparition, all coated with rain and floating on a bed of mist. Jared told us later that the Cadillac had screamed to a stop beside him and the guy inside, with a wild-haired, world-ending frenzy, had gone off about the storm, the wind, the thunder! Jared tried desperately to extract how far the campground was, but the wild-eyed storm-chaser was too terrorized to respond.

"Big storm! Tornadoes touching down!" he shouted.

"Where's the campground?" Jared asked.

"Trees flying—"

"Where's the campground?"

"Eighty-mile–an-hour—"

Jared grabbed him through the window by the collars of his Patagonia anorak and screamed, "How far to the damn campground!"

But the man just shrieked and blasted down the mountain with his wild hair flapping.

Jared didn't make it to camp—and neither did we.

Those distant thunderings were suddenly over the next hill, then the next rise, then *boom*, the loudest thundercrack since that night in Nebraska City, and the whole ocean came pouring down on our heads.

Jared waited for us at a fork in the road. He looked like a Dickensian orphan standing miserably in a downpour. *Which way to go?* We were all disoriented. Thunder was everywhere and rain came at us like shattered glass.

We went left and passed the Summit Lake Campground sign. On a little rise beneath a canopy of trees we pitched our tent and huddled inside. "This feels like a POW camp in the jungle," said Clint, who was reading all sorts of uplifting stories about prisoners of war. "Here's one ...This guy just got his legs blown off—"

"Clint, please."

"These are touching stories."

"Yes, Clint, but how many tales of pain and suffering can we take on one trip?" Clint had been filling us in on every gory detail since Nebraska.

The rain came down like it never intended to stop. And Clint, despite our protestations, was just too enthusiastic to shut up. So I stripped down and went outside and spread out on the picnic table and let it just drench me. If you can't beat 'em, join 'em, right?

"Hello, Mr. Rain. Thank you for this glorious drenching," I said. Then I started to bellow my rain song, as loud as I could:

Make the rain your buddy,
make the rain your pal.
You won't catch no cold
if you do what you're told
and you . . .
make the rain your pal!

"He's talking to himself again," they whispered in the tent.

"He always talks to himself."

"It's like this one guy—I just read the chapter—he goes insane, you know; he was ambushed—"

"For the *love*, Clint."

I felt for my fellow prisoners of war who didn't dare face the enemy on its own ground and terms, so after making love to the rain for a while, I began construction of my most ambitious project of the trip— a rain canopy.

I pulled the yellow tarp out of the Ark, assembled lines, cords, bottles, pans—all the raw materials, everything we had. Desperate for an escape from their muggy, Central American cell, Jared and Clint watched from a tiny slit in the front of the tent. I tied one cord to Clint's bike, one line to a hanging U-lock for balance and a rain escape, another couple ends to trees, pulled everything tight, balanced the torque, and just like that, we had a "hot chocolate shelter," as Jared called it. It was, without question, the engineering marvel of the trip.

"Is it dry?" Jared squeaked from the tent-cell.

"It is dry."

"Praise the Lord." Jared stumbled out of the tent and over to the table. "It's horrible, Daniel, horrible. He won't stop telling those Vietnam stories. And it really, really stinks in there."

Hours later, our books were piled high: *On the Road*, some Jacques Prévert French poetry, *Desert Solitaire*, *A Walk Across America*—fitting books for pilgrims. The storm cooled off and the moon came out for a brief cameo, and all the insects of the forest lifted their voices in blissful serenade. And we sat there as the campstove hissed, sipping hot chocolate, cup after cup, as we read and wrote and whispered (why, we didn't know), long, long into the night.

"If I hadn't gone back to pay for the gas, we would have made it to camp before the storm," whispered Jared, much later.

"Good thing you went back," I said.

43

The next day it was still raining. Our matches were soaked, so I struck off into the deserted campground hoping to find somebody with dry ones. There was one other camper hunched away in the trees. I knocked on the door and found four more POWs crowded around their little table under a dim, yellow bulb, playing cards.

"Will it ever stop?" I asked.

"Sometimes in West Virginia, it never stops."

They gave me a handful of matches and went back to their game.

Jared and I tried to get some True Fan Sludge going, but the stove was waterlogged. While I dried it off, Jared worked on "Country Roads" on the harmonica, and bless his heart, after about an hour of excruciating practice, he had it down pretty good.

I won't forget the moment that afternoon when the sun finally came back out. There is always a new, clean magic when a storm breaks, when the world's freshly baptized.

We had a word for this blessed sunlight in Scotland. There it *never* stopped raining, so whenever there was a hint of sun, we called it a Blue Eclipse and celebrated by stripping down in the nearest roundabout and soaking up every ray. Clint, fortunately, had missed that trip. But Micah, determined to beat the rain at its own gig, refused to wear shoes (he didn't even *bring* any), preferring to battle the elements in sandals. I guess *making the rain your buddy* only works so long, because after fifteen hundred miles the skin was peeling off his toes, pus was oozing from the cracks, and everything was swollen. You think the smell in our tent going across America was bad . . . Jared, four years from his MD, prescribed shoes. Micah reluctantly acquiesced. In Fort William he did a little jig in the street in his crisp, fresh socks and his happy, blue Pumas.

We got off late that afternoon, the sun still shining. But it wouldn't last. Twenty minutes later it was pouring down our faces and it followed us all through the next day, and the next.

Since the truce in Summit Lake, I was really enjoying the rain. Clint and Jared, but especially Clint, were not. While climbing one of our last mountains in West Virginia, Clint finally had had all he could take. He hadn't really lost it since the Fourth of July, so he was more than due.

"I'm sick of biking. I'm gonna throw my bike into the Atlantic Ocean." He tossed his bike off the side of the road and collapsed in the gravel. "We're doomed."

"Get up!" yelled Jared, hunched over his handlebars in exhaustion.

"Here it comes again, Clint," I said.

"Oh, I know. I've known that for a long time. It's gonna keep coming and it's not gonna stop."

"It's never going to stop," said Jared. "Never."

And with that Clint broke into this maniacal laugh that actually scared us a little bit. And he lay there laughing and laughing on the side of the road until, wouldn't you know it, it started raining again.

"Oh, and *these* things," he said with a betrayed, menacing tone in his voice a couple minutes later, sitting up and gently stroking the rain-beaded, NASA-designed rain-covers lovingly tucked over his panniers. "These *rain-covers* don't do a damn thing!" And he ripped them off in one motion, like tearing plastic produce bags off the dispenser in the grocery store.

Jared and I looked at each other in disbelief. "Congratulations on circumcising your panniers, Clint," said Jared.

Somehow we made it to the top of the pass. The town of Franklin lay on the other side. "I've never wanted a warm shower more in my life," said Clint. Jared agreed. Despite perpetually low funds, we pulled into a dingy motel and inquired about a room. The clerk took one look at us and told us they didn't have anything.

Ahh, well, we couldn't afford it anyway. We coasted into Franklin at dusk, cold, tired, and miserable.

"You know," said a woman pulling out of a 7-Eleven where we'd stopped for snacks, "the pastor of the Lutheran church just around the corner takes in folks like yourselves all the time. You should go there."

We took her advice, knocked on the door, and met soft-spoken Neil Wentzien who had no vacancy issues and immediately gave us free rein of the chapel basement for the night. There was a piano, kitchen, hot water, Ping-Pong table. It was unbelievable.

"You know," said Clint, lying on the floor, recovering from his mania, "I just feel like the rain is over. I feel like we've passed the trial, and now it will leave us alone." Oddly enough, we felt the same.

After settling in, I went upstairs and sat in the quiet hall, the stained glass blood-hued in the moonlight, shining above the altar. And I was suddenly so thankful for the trip, for my friends, even for my streaky efforts in trying to capture it all. In that moment, I didn't care. I embraced the struggle like I embraced the rain. I was doing my best, and somehow, it would be enough.

"God, I thank you," I said. I'd never meant it more.

44

"You know, when you're biking along, you, like, lose track of where you are, you know, and you think suddenly you're riding back home, back in Utah. But here we are in West Virginia. And it feels like . . . home. America has become our home."

We were sitting on a grassy hill, beneath a gigantic, old maple, beside a quiet church, deep in the mountain country. Jared had said these words, which all of us, in one way or another, had been thinking—or feeling. None of us knew exactly when it had happened, but somewhere between Los Angeles and West Virginia, America had become our home. It was a miracle in itself, that we could suddenly feel as comfortable on a nameless hill in the Appalachians as we did in Cache Valley.

Across the grass a wedding party was coming out of the church.

"Ahh, the rituals of life," I said.

Having been on the road for a while, we felt the gift of perspective settle over us. The gift of perspective is a pilgrim's ability to exist in a middle ground, not quite connected to the world but not apart from it. It's like you're watching life from the twilight, standing in a narrow corridor of illumination. You are a part of everything and nothing. You are a ghost and a god.

■　■　■

After surviving Cape Wrath, we biked down the cold, rainy, wild West-ern Coast of Scotland. Not many years ago, a ferry provided the only ac-cess to the Isle of Skye, but now, the fairy-tale Skye Bridge spans the kilometer-wide inlet. We saw the bridge in the distance, its delicate out-line suspended in the air. It looked like an illusion, a magician's trick that would fade away with the evening light. But the bridge was still there when we arrived, even as night crept over the water. As we rode across, we felt the island tug and strain on the bridge; we felt the steel girders flex and the cement bend and creak. No island likes to be tamed; per-haps this bridge was the only thing keeping Skye from floating away and joining Avalon.

Dusk hushed over the island. We found a grassy lot near Broadford and pitched the tents. Then a voice rose into the perfect still, a voice as rough-hewn and full of magic and legend as the broken-down moun-tains around us. The voice belonged to the lead singer of the Clansmen. He and his band were on tour and had the night off. He sang from his beat-up Impala on the other side of the grass. He sang to no one in par-ticular; he just sang to the night.

As he cried out in his ancient tongue, I went walking down the quiet road and that old, Celtic magic lifted the full moon over the scat-tered hills. It was so gigantic I thought it too was an illusion. The trans-parent light clarified the long fields and every blade of grass with perfect dimness, then ran down and whispered on the bay.

I kept walking, found a phone booth, made a call to an old friend far away who wasn't home. And when I stepped from the phone booth—the miracle. I don't know where it came from, but suddenly, the most glorious smell in the world was all around me—the smell of freshly washed women's hair.

Entranced, I walked into the middle of the road. Where is she, my Celtic princess? I fully expected her to appear. It reminded me of one evening, taking a walk with Melanee a few days after we met. She had that smell. It was like a thousand other evenings and moments and they all came rushing down like the Nebraska City downpour.

I stood in the middle of the road, drenched to the soul as the moon rose and the singer's voice cried out like a lonely phantom in the distance.

45

We had only one day on the Isle of Skye. As we sat around the next morning eating Sludge Cake and drinking tea, we discussed how we should spend it. There was a blue tourist bus that ran everybody up and down the coast at breakneck speeds—it cost sixteen pounds and gave you thirty minutes at Uig and fifteen minutes at Portrey, but according to the brochure, you saw *everything*. It was a sparkling Sunday morning and the magic of the previous night was still humming—though I could no longer catch the scent of freshly washed woman's hair, unfortunately.

We walked down to the bus stop, waited for the blue bus, got halfway on, and thus nearly sacrificed our will to a checklist, one of the most devastating decisions a pilgrim can make.

But at the last minute we looked up and saw a beautiful mountain slope fringed with heather.

"Let's climb the mountain," we said together.

We bought a slew of groceries, climbed into a meadow high above the bay, and there we passed the whole afternoon.

Far below us the blue bus came and went, carrying people from one end of the island to the other. "That could have been us," said Micah.

We talked and talked and ate cheese and crackers and drank Irn Bru by the liter. The afternoon was an eternity. And I realized as we lay there that somehow, magically, we had made it back to the Cavern of Wonders, back to a time of timelessness. It was as if we'd become gods, perched above the world to watch the people down below go scurrying about—trying to do everything, see everything, be everything—instead of just kicking back on a mountain slope and contemplating the heather, the wind, or that bug crawling across your McVittie.

The married couple in West Virginia and all their friends faded away. The gift of perspective carried us far and wide, east and west, future and past. The evening turned into a beautiful, wispy, spilled-milk sort of night. We drifted lazily in and out of sleep, talking for a bit, then falling silent for a long time.

46

A few days later we rolled through the mythical Shenandoah Valley into Harrisonburg, Virginia. We stopped at a Subway for some sandwiches and the fellow inside, a nice college student named Rick, took special interest in our quest. "You wanted extra meat with that sub, right?" He loaded it on without our responding and didn't charge us a dime more.

Outside a while later, we shot the breeze. "Listen, guys," he said, "why don't you come over to my place for the night. We don't got much, but you're welcome to whatever we got."

Rick lived in an apartment with three other students. One by one his pals poked their heads into the living room where we'd thrown out the bags and imparted their wisdom. The first roommate spoke of the benefits of "'shrooms," visions, and weed. The next roommate spoke of the benefits of girls, parties, and booze. Then Rick came and apologized for being a lousy host. "I'm sorry, guys; I'm just not feeling so great tonight . . . You know that girl you saw down at Subway? Well, she and I just broke up about an hour before you showed. We've been going out for three years."

That he would offer his hospitality during such an emotional period was testament to the guy's good heart. We needed to do something for him. It was time for us to attempt another Breakfast Shot.

"How much do you make at Subway?" I asked.

"I make minimum wage," he said. "It's really not worth it to work where I do."

"I'll tell you what. We're gonna get you a raise. The Subway World Headquarters is located somewhere in Connecticut—we'll just drop in on our way to the Hall of Fame."

Rick was thrilled and honestly believed we could pull it off. "It'd be great if I could make a couple more bucks."

"Now tell me your name again."

"Rick Linthicum."

"Linthi-what?"

"Let me spell it for you. I don't want some other idiot getting the raise; I want it."

47

Early in the evening of August 22, the day after Rick's place, we rolled into the Big Meadows Campground in Shenandoah National Park. Shenandoah snakes along for one hundred miles atop the last stand of mountains before the sea. The pilgrim sails over gentle undulations, gazing out over the Shenandoah Valley and an endless tumble of fields, forests, and ridges.

"This is some campground," said Clint as we took a walk around after pitching the tent. Hundreds of families were cooking up dinner, kids rode their bikes in endless games of tag, there were showers, phones, stores, laundromat! "What kind of camping is this?"

Curiosity the Bear would love this joint, I thought.

As we walked, we noticed a proliferation of BEWARE OF BEARS signs. We didn't realize there was a bear problem in the park, so we tracked down a ranger to get the skinny.

"Make noise when you hike, tie your food in trees, and stay in your tent at night," she advised.

"So," said Jared inquisitively, "how many people have been killed here by bears?" She thought for a second. "None, don't think." (This may be wrong, but it's what she told us.)

"How many mauled?"

"I don't think anybody's ever been mauled."

"Hurt, scratched, made fun of?"

"Once in a while a bear will chase a kid," she said. We imagined Boo Boo joining the bike-bound game of tag.

"My U-lock will not leave my hand," said Clint bravely, who had been sleeping with his theft-deterrent-slash-weapon every night since Amboy.

"Honestly," I said, "out West, we've got real bears, you know? Real claws, real attitudes, real reputations—not these picnic basket-stealing pretenders."

"I'm glad you're proud of your bears," she said. "I'm sure they're *very* scary."

And suddenly we realized, without our even knowing it, we had become just like everyone else we'd met! We too were practicing the "Be Scared" phenomenon!

"I could tell you stories about *real* bears," I said.

"I'm sure you could."

Bears like Old Ephraim, the last grizzly shot in Utah. Ephraim was a legend, a monster, eleven hundred pounds, ten feet tall, and wily as wily could be. It took rancher Frank Clark *twenty years* to catch this bear, setting traps all over the place, stalking him, ambushing him. In the meantime, Ephraim devoured hundreds of sheep, leaving a trail of carcasses across his massive territory covering much of Northern Utah and Southern Idaho, our home stomping grounds.

But Ephraim wasn't invincible, and after twenty years he finally made a mistake. One night he went for a plunge in his favorite, secret mud wallow and forgot to check for traps as he usually did. Clark had stumbled upon the wallow by accident the day before. The great bear had already been stuck with one trap a few years ago, but had managed to wriggle free—at the cost of a toe. This was how he got his nickname, "Old Three Toes." It's also one reason he was so difficult to catch. Once a bear survives the agony of a trap, he's going to be more careful next time. For more than a decade, the sight of that distinct, three-toed print in the mud or dirt sent shivers down the spines of every rancher in the Bear River Range.

Well, Ephraim blew it. He got his foot snagged. After a few minutes of rolling around desperately in the muck, he lurched out of the wallow and wailed down the canyon, dragging a fifteen-foot tree, connected to the chain, and the trap behind him. Clark heard him coming—probably everybody in the *West* heard him coming—got his gun, ran to the bottom of the draw (he had purposely camped a mile or so from the wallow), and waited for the bear to appear. After twenty years, this was it. One of them would die.

Suddenly Ephraim appeared on the trail about one hundred yards away. He took one look at Clark and put two and two together. This was the guy. Ephraim went mad. Clark shot six bullets into the great bear without making a dent. It was over for Clark, as Ephraim's massive, three-toed paw reared back to send Clark's head flinging like a pumpkin into the underbrush. But Clark had one bullet left, fired it at the last minute into Ephraim's skull, and leapt out of the way when he fell.

We toasted hot chocolate to our last night in the woods, and Jared made the most glorious Sludge of the trip. It was a Victory Sludge. "Nothing but metropolis ahead."

48

A few days later we found ourselves sitting at Lincoln's feet. We remembered the last time we'd seen him, striding out of New Salem, hardly comprehending the trials and miracles to come. Like Clint Eastwood in the film *In the Line of Fire*, we were eating ice cream cones. The sunlight was fading and we were gazing out over the mall.

Hours before we'd ridden into Washington, D.C., and arrived at the Lincoln Memorial. We hadn't moved since.

In those tranquil moments we were each struck with a new impression of the greatness of our country. From the sunny West Coast, across the desolate Mojave, down forgotten Route 66 where Steinbeck's ghosts crawled past us in their clanging monsters to the promised land, through the red rock country of Father Escalante, then the early summer mountains where wildflowers blushed beneath snowfields, on through the living green of the plains, the rolling Ohio Valley, the misty Appalachians, and finally, our nation's capital—every inch was connected.

The lights were coming on; the water in the pool reflected the serene, deep blue of the sky. We had no place to go, of course; and here we were stuck in the murder capital of the United States. Even Jared was unconcerned.

"Let's camp right here," I said. "Nothing bad could possibly happen to us beneath the gaze of Abraham Lincoln."

Jared shrugged; Clint shrugged. It was settled. We were camping for the night on the steps of the Lincoln Memorial. But then, like a heavenly apparition, the most beautiful girl we'd seen all trip glided up the steps thirty feet away. You spend three months on the road and everything is intensified, especially feminine beauty.

She happened to see us staring, and instead of ignoring us, came right over and invited us over for the night. Streaked with sweat and dirt and my hair wild, I looked like an ax murderer—or so some kid had said, warning his dad not to talk to me—but she didn't care. Her name was Sarah. Her roommate Jodi was equally accommodating. We followed them to their condo on Connecticut Avenue, hauled the bikes up four floors, and swapped stories until late. They even bought us pizza.

"I would love to do this someday," said Sarah. "We did a tour in Yellowstone a long time ago and that was fun, but to cross the whole country . . ." I could see the wheels in her head turning. And I remembered again the words of the wise bike shop owner: *"You will never know the effect you're having on the people around you . . ."*

Four years later, a five-year-old boy named Jordan Hargrave was on a family vacation with his parents. This time we were riding to the one place we'd never ridden before—home. Micah had rejoined us for the trek. The plan was to pull into Hyrum on the Fourth of July and ride in our hometown parade. We saw it as our last ride together for a while.

We ran into Jordan, his parents, brothers, and sisters at a scenic turnout near the majestic, snow-packed Mission Mountains in Northern Montana. Their van and camper were loaded with bikes and gear. They were on a family vacation from Post Falls, Idaho. It reminded us of our own family adventures, years and years ago.

The next day at a gas station, we ran into them again. "My son Jordan has something for you," said his dad.

And little Jordan Hargrave, of his own volition, had drawn each of us a picture of ourselves on our bikes, trusting he would run into us again. Beaming with pride, Jordan handed over the masterpieces. We were thrilled.

"You gonna ride across America someday?" I asked him. Jordan summoned a determined look and nodded profoundly.

"When we get to a campground," said Jordan's dad, "the first thing I do is pull out all the bikes. The kids go biking around for hours."

The next morning Sarah and Jodi served us oatmeal and signed the Ball, and we were off through the Eastern Seaboard. That afternoon we rounded an inlet of the Chesapeake Bay where we nodded to all the fishermen sitting on cardboard boxes on the broken-down wharf, gazing out with tired eyes across the gray confluence of river and sea, then through the heart of Baltimore and off into the suburbs where we camped in a park.

The next day we pulled through Philly, through some of the saddest slums we'd ever seen. We detoured out to the Spectrum so Clint could pay homage to the statue of Julius Irving (and here we found the celebrated Rocky statue, which had been quietly removed from the steps of the Philadelphia Art Museum a while ago). An hour later we biked downtown where we saw the fabled Rising Sun Chair, which has been around since Revolutionary War days and still sits in Independence Hall. Crafted in 1779 by John Folwell, the Rising Sun Chair was the chair George Washington used to sit in during an assembly.

"Does anyone ever sit in it now?" we asked one of the dressed-up guides after the tour.

"Nobody since Andrew Jackson," he said. Then he paused. "At least, that's what they'd like you to believe . . ."

He pulled us aside where nobody could overhear him. "You see, Ronald Reagan came through here one time, saw the chair, and before anybody could stop him, plopped right down. But what are you going to tell the President of the United States? Sorry, Mr. President, you can't sit there? Reagan sat there for a long time, just enjoying himself. He figured, heck, this is the Rising Sun Chair and I'm the president, so I should sit in it. After a while he got up. Everyone relaxed. No president has sat in it since."

That afternoon we crossed into New Jersey. While riding through Camden on a busy road through a bad part of town, a woman pulled up beside us, leaned out the window, and yelled, "Do you have a place to stay?" It was becoming comical the lengths Heroes around us were going to prove their Heroism.

Tammy McCoy and her friend Ava pulled over and gave us directions to Tammy's townhouse in Mt. Laurel. We cycled over.

"I've been waiting ten years, *ten years* to pick up bikers," she said. "When my friends and I went across America in eighty-seven, people were so nice to us, I've just been waitin' and waitin' to return the favor."

In the morning we struck off across New Jersey. We were so close to the ocean now, we felt it pulling us. And I saw in Clint's eyes a determination I had not seen all trip. I remembered his words to me in Vegas—that this was what he looked forward to most: hitting the Atlantic Ocean.

We rode through beautiful, pygmy forests in the heart of the state, then, as the sun dipped low, a stunning, double rainbow rose right out of the ocean. We rode across a bay into the town of Seaside Heights, then down the rain and sun-beaten roads where the sound of the waves was suddenly echoing in our ears. We rode right up to the place where the sand met the pavement, dropped the bikes, and ran leaping and yelling across the last stretch of land—one hundred yards of sand, then fifty, then ten—then right down into the foaming, crashing, inviting, celebrating ocean! I had never before seen Clint so recklessly happy.

The waves consumed us, and our cheers of joy, baptizing us of forty-four hundred miles of rain, sweat, grime, and effort.

50

The sun rose orange and enormous above the waves. Never had there been such a sunrise; no, not during ninety-two days from coast to coast. We had the feeling waking up that God had just dropped us there, on that stretch of beach, all alone. There was no past; there were no thoughts of the future. There was just the splendor of that sunrise, the purr of the waves.

We woke up slowly, as if from a long, deep dream.

Gradually the beach filled with people. Everybody gave us a tired glance as they passed by and forgot about us. They had other things on their mind. It was Labor Day weekend, the last gasp of summer.

No matter the final destination, to the cross-country pilgrim, the ocean is the *real* demarcation. It represents the pilgrim's accomplishment better than any point on the map. You can't bike any farther east if your life depended on it. And it is toward the ocean and the rising sun that you set your sights. No wonder Sal and friends always just turned around. What else were they going to do?

We found a café in the late morning and lounged around a table eating French bread. Newspapers shouted headlines. We felt eerily detached from whatever was going on in the real world. Somewhere, on some far-flung little planet, a princess had been killed.

"Last night," said Jared, "while we were running for the waves, I saw the whole trip flash before my eyes. The whole trip. And it was like one day had elapsed from the time we left Los Angeles to the time we got here, to the Atlantic Ocean. One day . . . And the day was over."

Clint was distant. The elation he had felt the night before had been replaced by an unusual solemnity. "It's depressing here," he said. "Nobody's doing anything. Like people are just dreading Tuesday, because not only is it the end of a three-day weekend, it's the symbolic end of the summer."

That afternoon Clint hopped on his bike with his basketball and a sad, helpless look on his face and disappeared. He left without a word; we could only guess that he'd gone looking for a basketball court where he could lose himself, a court where his dad would slip in the back and watch him shoot around until he felt better.

What do you do when you can't go east anymore? What do you do when you reach the top of the mountain, when you can't climb any higher? What do you do then?

"Look down there, Jare, look down the beach." He looked. It was strewn with people as far as we could see. It looked like the beach went on forever.

"Do you see it, Jare—do you see it?"

He squinted into the bright afternoon. "I see it."

"Let's walk there."

"OK."

When you come to the end of one journey, you begin another.

In the far, far distance, almost too far away to be real, spun a gigantic Ferris wheel perched high above the hot sand. It shimmered through the heat waves; it looked like a mirage.

"Is it real?" Jared asked.

"I don't know."

"How far away do you think it is?"

"I don't know."

We began to walk. It was like we were floating across the sand. We had grown more accustomed to moving than resting.

As we walked, little dramas played out around us. Here, a young family: boy with a jellyfish on a stick puts jellyfish down little sister's swimsuit. Not good for little boy. Many spankings. Here, a couple working out some sort of lovers' tiff: knee-deep in the waves he holds her hands, she pulls them away; he shakes his head and slaps the water with his palm. It's the same story told a thousand times over. The gift of perspective was upon us again. In the sky airplanes zoomed by, trailing banners. The hours passed, or so it seemed, and gradually the Ferris wheel drew closer.

We discussed everything we'd seen from coast to coast. We rehearsed everywhere we'd camped, everyone we'd met, every mountain pass and prairie sunset for four thousand miles. It was easy. We had complete recall. Even all these years later when we get together, my brother and I will go for long, long walks, just like that day on the beach, and rehearse everything that happened, for every single day going across America. We still remember.

Behind us now the beach stretched on to infinity. Our campsite was lost, our bikes, abandoned on the sand. We hadn't even thought to lock them up.

Closer and closer we came, and now we saw that the Ferris wheel spun on top of a boardwalk supported by stilts. We could see the water lapping between them; we could see all the kids lining up for their last chance to ride to the sun.

Beneath the boardwalk we walked, and here the stilts were encrusted with decades of barnacles. We looked up and saw the Ferris wheel shining and winking through the boardwalk, sunlight glinting off the metal and spinning down through the slats into the sea. The waves lapped ceaselessly and we heard the stilts creak and groan beneath the weight of the wheel. I wondered how long it would be before the stilts gave way and the great Ferris wheel crumbled into the sea like some gigantic jellyfish.

We walked back up the beach. By now, the mangled corpses of jelly-fish outnumbered people. The sun was getting low; the last gasp of sum-mer was just about spent.

When we finally got back to our modest shade structure (con-structed with the same yellow tarp I'd used for the far more successful hot chocolate shelter), Clint had returned.

"You found a court, didn't you."

He didn't even look at us, just spun the ball on his finger as he stared at the waves.

51

After another night falling asleep to wavesong—and convincing the local law enforcement to let us stay—we broke camp and biked along the coast through Ocean Beach and Point Pleasant until we found a park with a picnic table in nearby Neptune City. Clint had confided to me that we might just want to skip New York. Despite everything we'd seen, Jared was horrified.

"Why do we have to go to New York anyway?" Jared said that night by lantern glow. "The only thing binding us to New York is that stupid Summit Cologne."

"Honestly, Dan," said Clint, "I didn't think you were serious back in Colorado—"

"I told you I was serious."

"We could get killed," said Jared.

"We'll be fine."

"But why risk it? People die all the time in New York."

"Ten million people live there."

"Still, it's dangerous."

"Listen, Jare, how could we be protected from LA to the ocean, four thousand miles of sleeping in parks and crashing in fields, and not be protected now?"

"But that's different, Daniel—this is New York!"

"You sound like Luke in that scene in *Empire Strikes Back*," said Clint. "You know, when he can't lift the X-wing because he thinks it's too big and Yoda shows him that it's the same concept, same as lifting a rock."

"This isn't *Star Wars*, Clint."

"What it all comes down to is this: *What's New York to God?* Is it any more intimidating than Hershey, Nebraska?" Jared was quiet. "Besides, Jare, I'm going to need you to shoot. I can't do it myself. I need your help on this one."

We spread out the maps. "Tomorrow morning we get to Staten Island. The next day, we hit Manhattan."

"How do we get to Staten Island?"

"Looks like about the only way is the Outer Bridge."

"Can bikes get across?"

I looked at Clint. "I hope so."

That night something happened that had not happened all the way across the country: a cop kicked us out of a park. It was a real bummer, as we'd already secured half a dozen Mushroom sprinklers. We found a Methodist Church, but the lawn was sparse. Two houses down, a man unloaded groceries from his car. We asked him if he knew the pastor; in fact, he *was* the pastor.

"I'll have to check with the 'board' to see if you can sleep inside," he said.

But the board evidently didn't care, because the next thing you know he was serving us iced tea and popcorn and inviting us over for breakfast the next day.

The pastor signed the Ball.

We biked all day up the coast, riding along the deserted boardwalks of Asbury Park and rounding the Sandy Hook tip of New Jersey. Clint proclaimed that if we got out of New York alive, he was buying *Billy Joel's*

Greatest Hits: Volume 3 in celebration. Jared did not take this as the joke it was intended to be; instead, he seemed to be ticking off the last few hours of his life.

We pulled through Perth Amboy at 8 P.M. It was just getting dark and we only had a few more miles to go before we could find a campsite on Staten Island. Getting to the island, however, proved to be the problem. When we got to the Outer Bridge, we knew we could go no farther.

So far during our adventure we'd done some fairly treacherous stuff. Coming off Boulder Mountain in Southern Utah, I'd wanted to hit sixty miles per hour. Clint was ahead of me and we were both flying down the mountain road. Clint was ebbing over to the shoulder, however, and I knew if I yelled at him to stay in the middle of the lane he might jerk the handlebars and block my path. So I tucked, and with the Ark of the Covenant's extra hundred pounds pushing me with all it had, flew right past him, the wheel of the Ark missing his back wheel by inches.

The last thing I saw on my speedometer was fifty-seven; then a huge turn jumped out in front of me and I clamped down on my front brake—the back one had been disconnected because the wheel was out of true—and slowed just enough to navigate the turn. Had a car been coming up the opposite lane, the trip would have ended right there.

So we weren't pansies, but to attempt to bike the Outer Bridge would be suicide. Two narrow lanes crammed with screaming traffic, no shoulder, no bike lane, just walls of cement that would make a lovely mural of our smashed skulls if somebody couldn't avoid us. It was dark and nobody would think to look for cyclists. Even Clint, who'd defied traffic for hours on 285 on the Fourth of July, didn't dare mess with the Outer Bridge.

We collapsed on our handlebars. We knew what this meant. If we couldn't get across the bridge we wouldn't be able to meet with Calvin.

We'd have to go all the way around and we wouldn't have time. We were set to pull into the Hall of Fame on September 8, exactly one hundred days after our departure from Los Angeles. Getting across this bridge was everything.

"Well, that's too bad," said Jared.

"Wait," said Clint. "Over there." Two Port Authority police officers were getting some coffee at a 7-Eleven. We biked over and explained our dilemma.

"You see, if we don't get across this bridge, we won't be able to get to Manhattan—"

"And you won't get to pitch your cologne line," finished Officer Lee, a regal, black woman.

"What we really need is police escort across the bridge," said Clint bluntly.

The two cops looked at each other and burst into laughter. It was as ridiculous a request as turning off the foghorn.

"Strictly against code," chuckled Officer Lee.

"This is our one chance; we've got to get across this bridge!"

The officers just shook their heads.

"If there were any other way, we'd take it," I said, making a final pitch. "We've got to get to Calvin Klein to pitch our cologne line." Despite how inane it sounded, and despite Officer Lee's bemused initial reaction, the cops decided to confer.

"Give us a minute," said Officer Lee.

We stepped away and watched them chat. I looked at Jared, Jared at Clint, Clint at me. Suddenly, the incident represented something more than just getting across a bridge. It was a test of the philosophy we'd believed in our whole trip, the philosophy embraced with the miracle of the Hero's Ball way back in Utah the day before we left. Somehow, simply because it was what we *truly wanted*, we had to get across that bridge.

After a few minutes the cops returned. It didn't look good. "We're really sorry, guys," said Officer Lee, "but it's strictly against code to escort you across the bridge. We could get in some big trouble."

"We're sorry we can't help you," added Officer Serbo.

Our hearts sunk. At this late hour, our faith had failed.

"However," said Officer Lee slowly, "if we were to find you on the bridge, in, say, *two minutes*, it would be in our best interest to get you safely to the other side as quickly as possible." She couldn't fully suppress a little smile.

"The wisdom of Solomon," said Clint as we kicked our legs over our bikes.

We pedaled onto the highway and were immersed in the frenzy. We passed the NO PEDESTRIAN and NO BICYCLE signs and watched the massive cement walls squeeze down around us. There was no turning back now. Then the traffic hemmed us in on all sides and suddenly we were surrounded by screaming cars with headlights and horns blaring. What if the officers didn't come? What if they were late? What if they were kidding? But, as had been our rule, none of us looked back.

And suddenly, a squad car pulled in front of us, and another one behind, lights flashing, and Officer Serbo on the megaphone, in a faux tough-guy voice barked, "Just stay in the lane and keep pedaling!"

And oh, did we pedal! We pedaled our hearts out across that bridge, with half of Staten Island muddling along at twenty miles per hour behind us.

On the other side of the bridge I asked Officer Lee for a citation as a souvenir. She smiled and wrote me up a warning. "Thank you so much," I said. "But there's one more thing we'd like you to do for us . . ."

Officer Serbo and Officer Lee signed the Ball.

That night we camped on the lawn of a Catholic church with a Zeus-like statue of St. Peter out front. Years later I'd date a girl who grew up going to this very church. Her parents still attend. "They thought it was hilarious that you guys camped on their church lawn," she said, smiling her calm, beautiful smile that had melted more hearts than mine.

"I can't believe it," muttered Jared as we fell asleep. "We're camping in New York City."

"Tomorrow's the big day, guys; tomorrow's the day three pilgrims pitch Summit Cologne to a king."

52

Were it not for the fact that I was making a film, I really doubt Summit Cologne would have happened. Sometimes I thought the trip was getting all the attention, and sometimes the film, but when you come right down it, the two are one. Not at odds, but partnered up to enhance the entire experience. In real-life narrative filmmaking, this is the essential element—the oneness of pilgrimage and film.

We awoke the next morning to the sound of dress shoes clicking up the walk. A priest walked by, glanced at us, and kept walking. Thanks to an outdoor outlet, I was able to charge our one battery. We had three or four blank tapes left, and Jared and I had already formulated our shooting strategy the moment we set foot in Calvin's headquarters: *Do not turn off the camera.*

Despite mine and Clint's initial enthusiasm, by the time we hopped on the Staten Island Ferry and began to cruise through the fog, an eerie dread had descended. Perhaps it was the mist, so thick we couldn't even see the Statue of Liberty. Perhaps it was Jared's tangible fright. Every time I looked at him, he looked at me like: *Can we go back now? Isn't this close enough?*

The ferry pulled up to the dock, there was the rattle of chains, and we wheeled into Battery Park. "Well guys, we have arrived."

A bike messenger pulled up beside us. "You are too wide, man, too wide," referring to our trailer.

"You know what that is, pal?" said Jared. "That's the Ark of the Covenant. It can be as wide as it wants."

The biker took a drag on the end of his cigarette and tossed it away. "New York ain't like any other city you've ever been to. You remember that. You may think you've seen a city like New York, but I tell you right now, it ain't like nothin' else on earth!"

I'd dialed directory two days ago and found Calvin Klein's address. I hadn't even known for sure whether the CK headquarters were in New York until I'd made that call; I'd just assumed. For all I knew, they could have been in Paris.

"Two-oh-five West Thirty-ninth street," I said. Jared nodded. He had accepted his fate. He would just have to hope for survival. Clint was into his silent, military mode. There was a job to be done, and we were going to do it.

We wove all over town. Bike messengers gave us a good look over as they flew by. The flag flapped proudly, like it had all the way, and nobody gave us any grief. New Yorkers are among the most patriotic people on earth.

We found Calvin Klein's headquarters without a hitch. The place didn't look much different from any other building in Manhattan, aside from the fact that it oozed emaciated, beautiful people—like there was a factory inside spitting them out or something.

And now came a crucial moment: "Clint," I said, "I always envisioned all three of us going up, you know, but somebody's got to stay and watch the bikes, and I need Jared to shoot."

Clint nodded like a true soldier. "I'll watch the bikes," he said.

"Thanks, Clint."

"It's like this one lieutenant in Cambodia, his general asked him to stay behind and—"

Jared shot him a glare.

"Go see Calvin," Clint said.

Jared and I approached the main doors. A model in skintight Lycra breezed by—quite a contrast to our sweaty bodies, seawater hair, and tank tops. I pulled Jared aside. "Remember Jare, the One Rule—"

"*Don't turn off the camera.*"

"Right."

Just to make sure nobody could tell when we were shooting, we put a piece of black duct tape over the little red light. The camera had a handle on the top and Jared and I had already practiced *stealth shooting*, where he lowered the camera and looked away, but aimed it in the general direction. We had a full charge and fifty-seven minutes of blank tape.

The moment we walked through the double doors we were stopped by a gold-toothed guard. Was it over before it even began? He pulled us aside. "What are you guys doing?"

"We're heading up to see Calvin," I said.

"Sure you are."

"We just rode our bikes across the country. We got an idea for a cologne line in Colorado, and we wanna pitch it to Mr. Klein."

The man nodded quietly. He was a Jamaican fellow and comparisons to Kenny Shaw, our first hero, did not escape me.

"If you try to go up through here, you'll never make it looking like that. And the seventeenth floor, the executive offices, is secure access only. You won't make it."

"What should we do?"

"Well," he said, "if it were me, I'd run around back and take the freight elevator. Act like you know what you're doing, and go right up."

Unlike the front door, the gaping cavern accessing the freight elevator oozed not the beautiful and emaciated, but the slouched, the beer-bellied, the sunburned. We marched over to the elevator, the door opened up, we walked in, the elevator guy asked us which floor, we said seventeen, the door closed, and up we went.

Jared looked at me; I looked at him; the camera rolled. A couple people got on and off. And then it was just us. Fifteen, sixteen, seventeen. *Ding.* Door opens. We step out. Elevator closes behind us.

Jared and I are in a service corridor. We try the door; it's open. We walk in. We are in the executive offices of Calvin Klein.

Well, tank tops and basketball shorts were probably not the recommended attire, judging by the first few people we saw. But nobody gave us more than a glance. This was New York, after all. We wound our way through the offices and came at last to a reception area. We walked up to the desk where George, a guy who looked like a mafia hit man, was on the phone. He took one look at us, and, unlike everybody else, about hit the ceiling.

"How did you get in here?" he asked.

"We came up the freight elevator."

George shooed the camera aside. Jared went into stealth mode.

"Who opened the door for you?"

"It just opened by itself."

George picked up a phone.

"Can I explain myself?" I asked.

"Hold on. Hey, are you looking at the camera? I've got two guys here . . . They came up the freight elevator . . . Look at the camera! I can't—I'm up front here . . . Send somebody down." He lowered the phone. He was not amused.

"Can I explain myself?" I asked again. George nodded. "My friends and I—there's another one of us downstairs—we're on a cross-country bike trip. While we were coming over the Rockies we got an idea for a cologne line, which, I resolved, once we arrived in New York, we would pitch to Mr. Klein."

George only shook his head, still staring at us in disbelief. "You've got to get that in advance . . . You don't just walk in and go to see Calvin."

"Is there someone in the PR department that perhaps could help us out with this?"

It was the moment of decision—you could see it in his face. He had no reason to help us. But when you're on a pilgrimage, you come to expect the miraculous.

"Have a seat," he said.

For those of you unfamiliar with the upside of the underwear world, the offices of Calvin Klein are white. Everything is white, save for the black CALVIN KLEIN inscribed on the wall. This is why we looked so funny standing there in our filthy pilgrim gear—especially me, because I'd worn the same tank top since Venice Beach. And, true to what you might think, there were models everywhere. Models and beautiful people all done up perfectly.

While we got comfortable in our new digs, a couple more guys arrived on the scene. "Fellows, this is the head of security."

"Do you have an appointment?" he asked us.

"Uh, no," I said.

"They want to see Calvin," said George.

"Usually you have to get that months in advance."

"They've got this *cologne idea.*"

"How did you get in here?"

"We took the freight elevator."

"The freight elevator . . ."

"We're from Utah, from a little town of about three thousand people . . . We don't know how these big-city things work."

The security team thought this sounded reasonable enough.

"I don't mean to cause you guys any trouble—"

"Oh no, not at all!" said George. "You guys didn't do anything wrong—*we* did wrong. Breach of security. This is our fault."

"Give these guys to Kristen," said the security head to George. "OK, guys, George'll take care of you." We shook hands again and they took off. George wrote down a name and number for us.

"This is the number of Calvin Klein's personal assistant. Her name's Kristen. I can't guarantee this will work, but you can give her a call and explain your pitch."

It was unbelievable. Ten minutes ago we were a security breach—now everybody in the office was rooting for us.

I picked up the phone and punched in the number. But before I even had time to make the call, George had gone the extra mile *again* and appeared with Kristen at his side.

"This is the assistant," he said. We told Kristen the whole story.

"Are you looking for corporate sponsorship?"

"We're not looking for money or anything like that," I said. "All we want to do is follow through with a magical scenario envisioned two thousand miles back." She looked at George. George leaked his own smile of amusement.

She took out a pen and went over to the counter to write something. I turned to George, our new confidant and fellow True Fan. "If we could just pull this off, that would be a magical moment, you know ... it would be really magical." George nodded right along with us.

"Well," said Kristen, returning from the desk, "it's not going to be magical right now." She handed me the paper with her name and number. "Write up some information, tell us what you want, what you're doing, that you just rode your bikes across the country . . . I'll see that Mr. Klein gets it. Maybe something can happen."

I took the paper and thanked her. It wasn't a meeting, but you know, it wasn't bad. "Have a safe trip," added Kristen.

53

George escorted us back to the freight elevator. "Thanks for your help, George." He nodded as the doors closed in front of us. We walked back out to the street where Clint stood with his arms crossed, watching the bikes.

"Clint!" He spun around. "We came that close!"

We told him the story. "Her name's Kristen, she even gave me her number . . . So, we're past first base—we're doing OK! Summit cologne just may live!"

Invigorated and transformed, Jared handed the camera to me. "We marched right up, no fear, walked right into the executive offices . . . and almost got to him."

Clint was anxious to scale the Empire State Building, but first we had to run over to Kinko's and type up a letter. I dropped it off in the lobby downstairs and nodded at the gold-toothed guard.

Then we biked over to the gigantic skyscraper. The moment Jared and Clint entered the building (I stayed and watched the bikes this time), the head of security pulled them aside, asked them what they were doing, and, after hearing their story, rushed them to the top for free. He cut through a huge line and saved them twenty bucks and a forty-five minute wait. He did the same for me when they came back down.

We spent the night in the Chelsea Youth Hostel, packing new friends Lars and Carrie into our tiny cubbyhole, along with our bikes and gear. Lars and Carrie were stiffed out of a reservation and stuck with no place to stay for the night. Their story sounded familiar, so we invited them to stay with us. We went to a Mets game, Carrie bought everybody the best hot dogs of our lives, and the next day we prepared to leave. Clint desperately wanted to shave, but I begged him to hold off.

"Clint, we gotta look like pilgrims when we get to the Hall of Fame!"

"That won't be hard," said Jared.

"Yeah, but if you shave, it will destroy the effect."

"You're not shaving, right, Jared?"

"Nah."

Clint looked at me, disgusted, then stormed off. Jared, Lars, Carrie, and I sat around the picnic table debating whether or not Clint would shave. Carrie thought he would; so did Lars. Jared and I knew differently. "Clint's really into this all-for-one-and-one-for-all thing. He's in the military, he's been reading war stories all trip. If Jared and I don't shave, he doesn't shave either."

Fifteen minutes later Clint appeared, freshly showered with a week's scruff still clinging to his face. "Unless I'm captured as a prisoner of war," he said, "this is the longest you will ever see my facial hair."

54

We left New York later that morning on Route 1. A man walking down the sidewalk in the Bronx yelled after us, "Where you goin'?"

"The Basketball Hall of Fame!" we yelled back.

"Where you bikin' from?"

"Los Angeles!"

At this, the man let out a joyful whoop. "Well, you just keep on ridin'! Keep on ridin'!"

Little kids ran along beside us, proclaiming that someday, they would bike out West to see *us*. We passed famous courts where the best of the best competed between chain-link fences, beneath high-rise apartments. You play every day on a court like this and it's no wonder you get to be Isiah Thomas or Allen Iverson. But then again, there are many ways to achieve greatness.

A far cry from the 110th Street courts, Steve Stockton, John Stockton's older brother, showed us the garage door hoop in Spokane where he and John used to battle it out. "To this day," said Steve, "I can't go left." That's because there's a wooden fence hemming you in. Steve had stopped by to welcome us to Spokane after our first pilgrimage and offered to show us around.

"We had some pretty mean battles," said Steve. Their motivation wasn't the concrete jungle around them and the best competition from West 4th to Harlem; their motivation came from a different source.

"You see that building right across the street?" We turned around to look. "That's a Catholic girls' school." He smiled, as if a great secret had just been leaked. "When you've got hundreds of girls staring at you every day from their dorm rooms, you play *hard*."

We passed through the rest of the Bronx, marveling at how extensive the city was, and then marveling again when the city abruptly transformed and we entered Fairfield County, Connecticut, one of the richest counties in America. We biked all the way to Stamford, dropped in at the World Wrestling Federation headquarters for some reason, then found a nice perch in a lonely park where we could sit on the rocks and look out across the Sound at the skyscrapers beyond. The noise of Manhattan had faded into the gentle lap of waves. And suddenly all was peaceful. In the madness escaping the city, this was our first chance to kick back and think. Bike thieves, murderers, and psychotic bike messengers notwithstanding, we had come through New York alive.

55

And so we just sat there on the rocks—rocks that pilgrims had stood upon, Algonquin children had probably played upon, explorers wondered upon, lovers spoken upon, of their lives together; rocks that storms had splashed with saltwater and the sun had dried, over and over again through the centuries. The sun was getting low, the air was cool, and a perfect peace had stolen over us. It was a different sort of peace than the one we had felt on the seashore; it was more substantial. Perhaps it was OK now that the journey was coming to an end. Instead of a feeling of helplessness, there was a feeling of empowerment.

Having conquered cities, hit miracle shots, infiltrated palaces, requested audiences with kings, crossed uncrossable bridges, baptized ourselves in rivers and oceans, quested to the very roots of Heroism, and pedaled over four thousand miles, we felt we could pretty much do anything. And so we just sat there calmly, waiting for the next miracle to rain down from heaven, whatever it might be.

"Are you willing to wait for the miracle?" Marc Cohn asks. But usually you don't even have to do that.

Fifteen minutes later a guy jogged by, asked us what we were up to, and invited us over for the night. George was a FedEx driver who had pilgrimage aspirations of his own one day. He bought us pizza, we swam in his pool, and he signed the Ball the next morning.

Then it was on to Boston, and now we had to hurry; we had three days left to get to the Hall of Fame. We could easily make it if we went straight north to Springfield, but there were a couple items of unfinished business; the first was Subway.

Back in Harrisonburg, Virginia, Rick Linthicum was still toiling away, making sandwiches for five bucks an hour, trying to get through school and romance his way back together with his girlfriend. Rick was counting on us.

We found the Subway World Headquarters tucked away in the town of Milford, Connecticut. We rode right up to the front doors like the Visigoths to Rome, dumped the bikes, and walked in. I didn't need to rehearse the One Rule to Jared; by now, he was a pro.

We were instantly accosted by the receptionist who demanded we turn off the camera before she'd talk to us.

"You see, we met this guy—"

"Turn off the camera."

"—and we told him when we got here—"

"Off."

"—we'd see if—"

"*Off!*"

Jared lowered the camera to his side. The receptionist was still suspicious.

"You're pointing it right at me; is it off?"

"You don't see a little red light, do you?"

"Well, no."

"If the camera were on, you'd see a little red light. Everybody knows that."

Clint and Jared nodded.

The receptionist made a call. Her call was to security, but someone else had overheard our plea. Not two minutes later, Dick Pilchen, Subway's vice president, arrived on the scene. He immediately agreed to have a chat, much to the disbelief and disdain of the gatekeeper. As he would tell us later, he was Subway's oldest employee, in with Fred DeLuca on the ground floor thirty some-odd years ago.

Dick sat down with us and heard our spiel. He asked us all about our trip, the things we'd seen and done. "There was one night," I said, "we were struggling up this pass in Colorado—starving, you know—and when we got to the top, there's a Subway. Saved our lives."

"Monarch Pass," said Dick. "Highest Subway in the world."

We told him about Rick, his kindness, and our promise to get him a raise. Dick handed me a pen. I wrote down his name and the city in which he worked. Dick promised to get somebody on it. Rick would get his raise.

56

Over the next couple days we biked along the Connecticut coast, through the charming coastal towns of New London and Mystic, and pulled into Boston on September sixth.

"Cheers is the number-one tourist attraction in Boston," somebody told us, "ahead of Paul Revere's house, Bunker Hill, and even the Freedom Walk."

Upstairs in the landmark bar, we crashed root beers. Our waitress Kerry told the manager all about our adventure. He came out and promised us free dinners. We were exuberant—and relieved. Funds were low, and the fifty-dollar booklet of free sub certificates we'd been given in Milford was already half gone.

After the celebrations, we got up to leave and found a bill sitting on the table. We thought it was misplaced and just left. Outside, a disconsolate Kerry approached us. "Guys, I didn't find the money for the bill."

"We thought it was a mistake," I explained. "Your boss promised us free dinners."

"I think he meant that just the burgers were free," she said.

We couldn't believe it. Since when did "free dinner" mean, simply, "free burgers?"

"What's wrong, guys—don't you have the money?"

"We really don't," I said. "We figured it would be free."

"I'll talk to him," she said. Kerry disappeared inside and we lightened up. Surely it was just a little misunderstanding. But when Kerry returned it was the same story. "He says he can't do that."

Looking back, twenty bucks seems like a trivial sum, especially between the three of us, but that just goes to show how poor we really were. We were going to roll into Springfield on bread crumbs—and any True Fan Sludge Fixin's we could scrape out of the bottom of the Ark of the Covenant.

"I've got an idea," said Kerry. She disappeared inside again. We waited. A few minutes later she came back out. "It's all taken care of," she said.

"Your boss wrote it off?"

"No . . . Listen guys, I know you don't have a lot of money, and I know you thought it was going to be free . . . So I went around to a couple of my friends and borrowed twenty bucks. I'll pay them back when I get the money."

Kerry Coyne signed the Ball.

We wheeled our bikes across the street to the Boston Common. "I think that was one of the most sincere acts of kindness we've seen so far," said Jared as we entered the Common, America's oldest park. Kerry was going to school at Boston College and waiting tables at night. She, too, was pinching every penny—but she paid our bill ahead of her own.

We found the widest, most open field of grass, dropped the bikes, and fanned out with our heads together like the spokes of a wheel.

The city rose above us, the sounds of the city rose around us; we had no fear. We were beyond fear now. And very slowly, after many long conversations, we fell asleep.

The next morning Jared walked down to a little pond where ducks and ducklings waddled and splashed into the sunlit waters. He was so relieved to have survived the murderers, bike thieves, drunk drivers, UFOs, gangsters, mafia bosses, tornados, Winnebagos, giant spiders, and desert hermits, that all he could do was play "Amazing Grace" on his harmonica again and again.

He's never played so well.

57

Later that day we found our way over to the King's Chapel. We looked pitiful, still in our tank tops and coated with sweat. But that didn't stop an exuberant greeter in a blue suit from knifing through the crowd and inviting us to the service as if we were the long-awaited guests of honor.

Inside, the pastor opened his remarks with the following: "We'd like to extend a special welcome to Dan, Jared, and Clinton, three guys biking from Los Angeles. I just think the world's a better place when people are walking or biking across the country."

What a nice thing to say! But how exactly *was* the world a better place? We hadn't done anything overtly spectacular. How was the world a better place when people went on pilgrimages simply for the joy of it?

There's this little rule we use to make decisions; we call it the Universal Joy Principle. When making decisions it is wise to consider which decision will pump the most amount of joy into the universe. If the universe will have more joy if my brother and his six buddies borrow my van for a weeklong road trip, they get the van. If, however, more joy will be generated in the universe if I keep the van so I can take out this girl I've had a monster crush on for months, then I keep the van. (It would have to be *some* girl; my brother and his friends generate a lot of joy.) Eighteenth-century Scottish philosopher Francis Hutcheson put it this way: "... *action is best which produces the greatest happiness for the greatest number.*"

My friend Suzy really took to the theory; at her wedding reception five years after our trip across America, her friends confided in me that she had abused the Universal Joy Principle by saying that "that skirt looks better on me than you, so, according to Dan Austin, I keep it."

"I lost more clothes that way," said bridesmaid Julie. "Thanks a lot, Dan."

By going on the trip, more joy had been generated in the universe than had we stayed home.

For another thing, we believed from the start that everyone wants to be a hero. This doesn't necessarily mean rescuing infants; it simply means being true to oneself. I thought about the PowerAdes in the desert, about Louise Parsons, about the waitresses in Glen Ferris. I thought about Tammy McCoy who'd finally found her pilgrims.

Just the other day I got a call from Anthony, a kid from Pennsylvania who saw *True Fans* on the Banff Mountain Film Festival World Tour, vowed to bike across America, and three years later was hitting every fire station from Philly to Frisco with his buddy Shawn. Among other tidbits, they included a "Dog Chases to Date" column on their daily e-mail updates.

It seems that somehow going on a pilgrimage for nothing more than the sheer joy of it *does* make the world a better place. You become a cog in the miraculous Cycle of Heroism, accepting Heroism from some, and in so doing elevating them to Heroes—True Fans—and then passing that Heroism on in your own way. "Heroic karma," I guess you could call it. The only prerequisite to this Hero-making power is that you go on the journey because *you truly want to.* The journey itself becomes an act of Heroic Expression, an act, which, if approached with the intent, enthusiasm, and commitment of a True Fan, will make you and those around you into Heroes.

How does this happen? What is the process of this miracle? "*The heart becomes heroic through passion,*" answers Victor Hugo.

We had come to find during our journey across America that Heroic Expression takes many forms. A miner can practice it through his mining. A chef can practice it through her cooking. A reverend practices it; so does a caretaker, a Pilgrim, a trailblazer, a pioneer, a farmer, an architect, a biologist, a mathematician, a songwriter, a soccer coach, a filmmaker.

No matter the act, the result of Heroic Expression is always the same: *It will set you free.*

There are Heroic Acts of *creation*, like figuring out an algorithm or directing a play. There are Heroic Acts of *love*, caring for someone or something purely, heroically. And there are Heroic Acts of *seeking* in which your journey itself is *Go neiri an bothar leat* in motion.

But every act of Heroic Expression is a journey when you get right down to it—a pilgrimage to your Heroic Identity, from Caretaker to Reverend—whether you physically go anywhere or not.

Every Heroic Act is equal, no matter how grand or humble. The widow's mite, after all, trumped them all. Whether you're Jack Kerouac, the Postcard Seller, Richard Bennett, or a million other Heroes, sung and unsung, across this great nation of ours, and all over the world: every Heroic Act is equal.

"You can't pray a lie," reasoned Huck Finn as he and Jim floated down the river on their own pilgrimage—and you can't shoot one either. You probably can't even *bike* a lie. I don't believe Clint's Breakfast Shot would have had a chance in a million of going in if basketball weren't his own beloved form of Heroic Expression.

We chatted with folks outside the chapel after services and were on our way by the early afternoon. We biked to Worcester and camped on a grassy hill. I don't think we realized then just how much we'd look back on those times and long for them with all our hearts. Clint wrote a long letter to a girl back home. I think, in fact, it was Lisa, who never truly exited the radar screen, even after ten years of pursuit.

"No matter what happens at the Hall of Fame tomorrow," I said, "it has been the very best trip of my life, with the very best friends a guy could have, and nothing, *nothing* will diminish that." But I didn't need to say a thing; there was no doubt what would happen tomorrow, the only thing—*the best thing*.

In the morning we packed up our bikes for the last time and began the final leg to the Basketball Hall of Fame.

58

It was a rainy day. I don't think Jared and I really cared, but Clint was hoping for sunshine to finish off the trip. Fortunately his rain covers could no longer slow us down. Much to my disappointment, the rain washed us off—we weren't going to look quite as awful as I'd hoped.

We stopped at a gas station about halfway there and picked up a copy of the *Springfield Union-News*. And sure enough, front page, there was our article. An AP photographer had caught up to us in New London and taken a few pictures of the Hero's Ball and our gear. The story, which I'd been phoning in to Diane Lederman at the *News* in four increments going across, would be the Hall of Fame's only introduction to our tale. We hadn't called them; this wasn't a publicity stunt, after all, it was a pilgrimage. We were banking on the fact that somebody would see it, and the Powers-that-Be would be waiting for us when we arrived.

Clouds hung low and the rain fell off and on for the next two hours. On the outskirts of town we hit the Friendly's Ice Cream Headquarters and were treated to as much ice cream as we could eat.

Then we cruised into Springfield, legendary wellspring of hoops. A truck pulled up beside us and Charles Scott rolled down the window. "You're the guys—the biker guys!" he said.

"Which way to the Hall of Fame?" we asked.

"You just keep heading straight, go under the freeway, and take a left on Columbus. I'll meet you there!"

We rode under the freeway and rounded a corner and there was the mighty Hall itself, the resting place of heroes, Mount Olympus of hoops. Clint clasped his hands and cheered like he'd just won the championship. Jared and I exchanged a satisfied nod. We pulled into the parking lot and coasted up to the front entrance. Then, for the last time in forty-eight hundred miles, we hopped off our bikes.

59

In 1891 James Naismith was a physical education instructor at the Springfield School of Christian Workers. He was given the task of coming up with a sport that his unruly students could play indoors during the long, New England winters. After two weeks of frustration, he pinned a peach basket to each end of a rectangular court in the YMCA, came up with thirteen original rules, and thus, basketball was born. The only reason basketball hoops all over the world stand at a regulation ten feet is because that's how high the catwalk running track was to which Naismith pinned the baskets.

Despite the instant popularity of a sport that would come to attract hundreds of millions of participants, Naismith never became rich, or particularly famous. In fact, following a visit to Berlin in 1936 to witness basketball's introduction as an Olympic event, a tobacco company offered him six figures to become a spokesman. Naismith turned them down, believing that tobacco was detrimental to youth.

"So where is this first YMCA?" Clint asked Charles, the only person waiting for us when we arrived. "I've been dreaming about taking a shot on the *first hoop* all trip."

"Well, you passed it," said Charles.

"Passed it? That's impossible. I was looking for it the whole way—we would have noticed."

"No, you passed it," he said again.

"Where was it?"

Charles chuckled. "The YMCA where Dr. Naismith invented basketball was torn down a long time ago. A McDonald's sits on the very spot. You rode right by and didn't even know."

Clint looked like he was going to kill somebody. "They built a *McDonald's* . . . on top of the *first hoop?*"

Charles Scott nodded reverently. "People have talked about reconstructing it, buying back the land or something. But right now the only thing you can do on the site of the first hoop is buy a hamburger."

About this time the doors to the Hall of Fame opened. Heaven had produced an emissary; his name was Craig Fink, the associate director of PR.

"You're the guys, aren't you?" he said.

"We're the True Fans," said Jare.

"Welcome to Springfield. Welcome to the Basketball Hall of Fame. We saw the article in the paper this morning and wondered if you guys were for real. And just now I was looking out my window, and there you were. How was the trip?"

All of us just smiled.

"Guys," I said. It was time for the final ritual. I handed the camera to Jared, opened the Ark, pulled out the canvas bag hidden away deep inside, untied the drawstrings, and withdrew the Hero's Ball.

I handed the Ball and a Sharpie to Clint. He took them both with gusto, forgetting all about the tragedy of the first hoop. It was time to make new mythos. Clint signed his name and handed the Ball to Jared. I took the camera as Jared signed his name. Then I handed the camera back to Jared and signed my own name on the virgin leather.

The three of us took our places next to Chuck Glaze, Josh the Second, Sarah and Jodi, and all the other True Fans, coast-to-coast, who had helped us out, inspired us, pushed us along or lifted us up.

"We brought this Ball across the country," I said, "signed by Heroes, all across this great country of ours. And we were hoping, when we arrived at the Basketball Hall of Fame, that it would be enshrined, in this shrine for Heroes, as a token of humanity—a symbol of America, brought across America on the back of our bikes. What is the possibility of this happening?"

Craig thought for a moment. "My first reaction to it is that this Ball belongs in the same kind of category as the Ball that went on the first space shuttle flight. That Ball made a unique journey, and this Ball has made that same kind of unique journey." He turned the Ball over in his hands, looking at all the signatures, the stories.

"And so," Craig continued, "on behalf of the Basketball Hall of Fame, I'd like to accept this Ball for enshrinement. It will go on display and become a prized part of our collection."

60

We toured the Hall of Fame, met the brass, recited the trip a few times, loaded up on free T-shirts, shorts, and souvenirs, compliments of the Hall, did an interview for the local newspaper, and then decided we'd better find a place to camp. I was exhausted in every way from the trip, and had pretty much packed it in for good.

"Guys, let's just camp right here on the lawn of the Hall of Fame."

Jared didn't seem to mind. Clint, however, had other plans. He disappeared on his bike without saying a word, just like that day on the beach in New Jersey, and ten minutes later came whirling back, singing "We Are the Kings!" (one of our trip anthems) at the top of his lungs.

"Guys, I stopped in at the Springfield Sheraton, nicest hotel in town. I told the manager what we were doing, showed him the article, and he knocked a hundred bucks off a room—it's practically free! You don't just bike the country and then sleep on the lawn—you go out in style!"

Epilogue

There is a chilly lake in Montana just outside West Yellowstone called Hebgen. During the summer it is a popular destination for fishermen, campers, and boaters; during the winter, however, Hebgen is forgotten. It is not uncommon for the West Yellowstone area to log the coldest temperatures in the continental United States. This is enough to keep most people away.

A few weeks after the end of the trip, after we took a Greyhound back across America and swapped stories with an old driver as we crawled up into the Rockies—a driver who'd driven two million miles without even a fender bender, crediting "the angels"—I had retreated, alone, to the shores of this lake to think. It was October.

At first, it was horribly lonely being without my friends for the first time in months. I sat down at a deserted picnic table and fired up the campstove for a solo batch of Sludge, and a single mug of hot chocolate. It seemed impossible to me that they weren't there; at times it had felt that the trip would never end.

Jared was a sophomore at Utah State University. Clint was still set on piloting a nuclear sub. I didn't know what I was going to do . . . so I drove north. I got to West Yellowstone. I liked it. I got a job at a hotel, and lived on the shores of the lake. During the day I worked, and during the night, I camped.

I set up my tent thirty feet from the water. Inside, I piled blankets to the ceiling. Outside, snow covered the empty campground and turned the tent into an igloo.

Every morning mist hung in scarves across the surface of the lake, veiling the opposite shore. Sandhill cranes called from the obscurity. One morning when I opened my tent flap and gazed across the waters, I knew it was time to take a little dip.

The water was ice. I could feel my feet numbing up the moment I stepped in. A light snow was falling. I remembered my empowering baptism in the Mississippi River more than two months ago. Much to Jared's disbelief I never contracted malaria—but from somewhere not too far away I could hear him warning me now about hypothermia.

There's always a time after every pilgrimage when the world goes quiet, when the pilgrim is left to readjust, to come back to the surface of living like a deep-sea diver.

I caught the snow on my face as it drifted through the mist. For the first time in my life I had no plan and no direction—I simply had to trust that the future would take care of itself. For now, I was going to camp on the lakeshore, work for the hotel, and watch winter creep over Yellowstone.

I let myself fall back into the ice water.

■   ■   ■

THE END

True Fan Sludge

from SludgeMaster Jared

Invented June 2, 1997 in Rancho Cucamonga, California with multiple varia-tions on subsequent adventures, and ever in the process of continual revision.

←Sludge

←Campstove

DIRECTIONS:

In a large stew pot bring 3 liters of waters (3–4 standard water bottles) to boil.
Then add:

1-2 cups of uncooked rice (not the instant, nutritionally deficient crap). Simmer for 10 minutes.
Then add:

1-2 Lipton Instant chicken noodle soup packets, quantity added dependant upon availability and desired taste...

and

1-3 cups of curly roni, wagonwheel, fusilli, spirochaete, farfalle, gemelli, radiators, pipe rigate, orecchiette or any other type of

pasta (though preferably not spaghetti or linguini). Add the pasta so that the level of the pasta falls about **1/2 inch** below the water level of the pot in order to provide the desired **sludge-like consistency** of the finished product. Let boil with frequent stirring for another **10 minutes** or until pasta is done. Season with **salt, pepper** or whatever condiments are left over from the last condiment raid. Then serve up. The Sludge will initially scoop up like a **thick stew**, but after sitting overnight, it will become a congealed mass (**SludgeCake**) to be eaten for breakfast in the morning!

One may add cheese, tuna fish, tubers, Vienna sausage or other tasty additions to the basic Sludge recipe.

Basic recipe provides around **700 calories**, mostly from carbohydrates, per heaping serving (about 2 cups). Usual adventurer serving size 4–5 cups.

THE TRUE FAN GUIDE to SPRINKLER DISARMAMENT

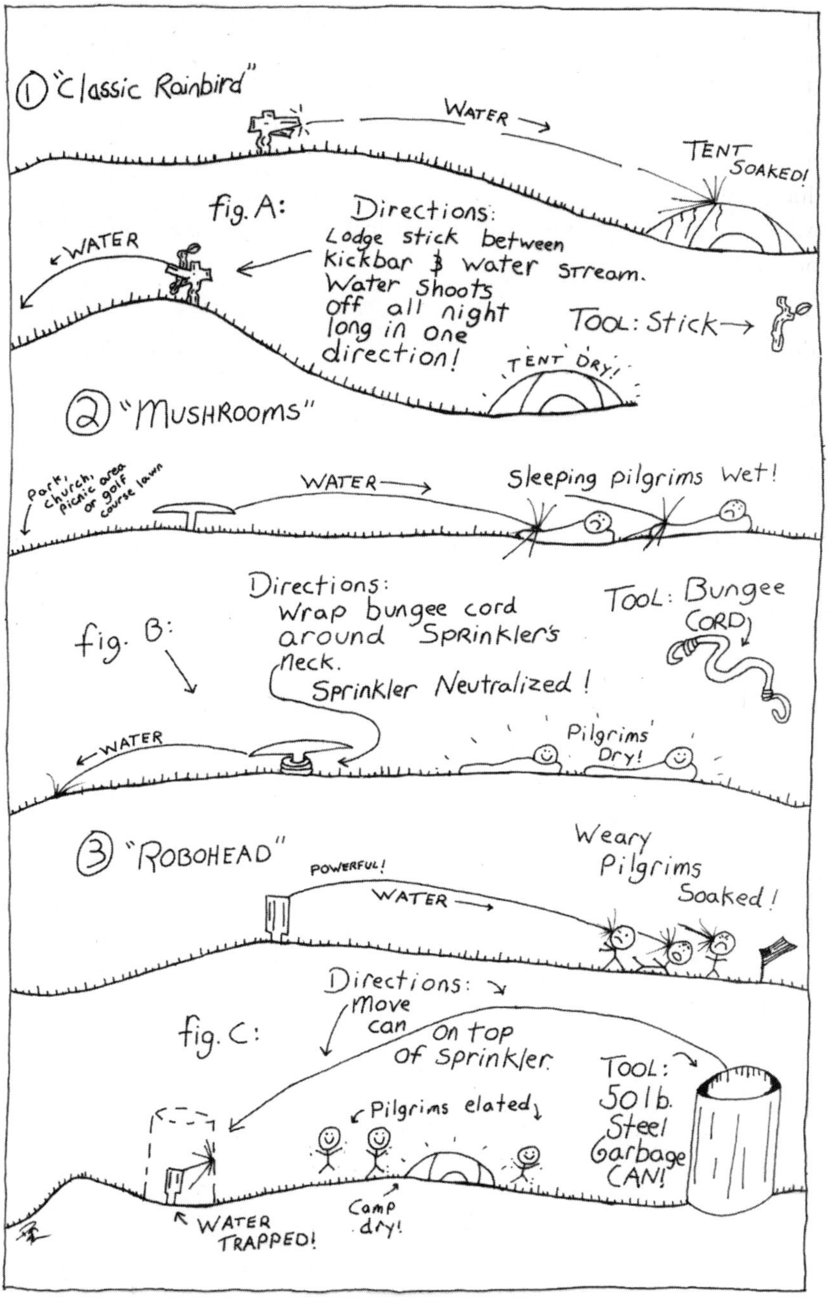